Letters from the Editor

Lessons on Journalism and Life

Letters from the Editor

Lessons on Journalism and Life

William F. Woo

Edited with an Introduction by Philip Meyer

University of Missouri Press
Columbia and London

Library of Congress Cataloging-in-Publication Data

Woo, William F., 1936–2006.
    Letters from the editor : lessons on journalism and life /
William F. Woo ; edited with an Introduction by Philip Meyer.
        p. cm.
    Summary: "A collection of essays by the first person outside
the Pulitzer family to edit the *St. Louis Post-Dispatch* and the
first Asian American to edit a major American newspaper.
William F. Woo touches on a wide range of subjects to inspire
the next generation of journalists"—Provided by publisher.
    Includes index.
    ISBN-13: 978-0-8262-1750-9 (hard cover: alk. paper)
    ISBN-13: 978-0-8262-1755-4 (pbk.: alk. paper)
    1. Journalism.   I. Meyer, Philip.   II. Title.
    PN4733.W66 2007
    070.4'1092—dc22
    [B]
                                                2007014951

∞™ This paper meets the requirements of the
American National Standard for Permanence of Paper
for Printed Library Materials, Z39.48, 1984.

Designer: Stephanie Foley
Typesetter: The Composing Room of Michigan, Inc.
Printer and binder: Thomson-Shore, Inc.
Typefaces: Matrix and Minion

To journalism students everywhere,
the next keepers of the trust.

Contents

Part III. The Obligations of Journalism

Foreword

O ne autumn evening in 1961, as I reveled in my new job as a copy
boy at the *Kansas City Times,* I made one of those inexplicable
mistakes, an error so elementary yet so typical of the kinds of
missteps we can make when we're young. Through a lapse in judgment,
I had run afoul of the city editor, Ray Lyle, a crusty, curmudgeonly figure, whose personality was probably too extreme to be believable in any
movie about journalism today. Lyle intimidated everyone by his fierce
passions for gathering and reporting the news: Everything had to be
done just right, and all the copy boys lived in fear of making a mistake.
On this night I had neglected to immediately give him an urgent call
from our police reporter. Lyle jumped all over me, incredulous that I
could be so stupid. I was shattered. My goal was to be promoted to a reporter, and this looked like a fatal setback. At a moment when it counted, I hadn't been able to cut it. Crushed, I retreated to the supply room,
where a few moments later I heard a soft voice behind me, saying, "Don't
worry, Jimmy. He'll forget about it." As he reached for a notepad, the vis-
itor flashed me a smile I would come to know over the years, reassuring
me that everything would be OK.

That was my formal introduction to Bill Woo. I'd been fascinated by
Bill since I'd arrived at the *Times* just two weeks earlier. It wasn't just the
presence of an Asian American in the newsroom that made him stand
out. Watching him come back from some mundane assignment and
transform the event into a gem of a story was magical. Whether he was
covering the arrival of the circus, reporting the death of a politician, or
capturing the subtle currents swirling through a civic meeting, Bill could
do it all, seemingly without effort. Early on, like just about everyone else
in the newsroom, young and old, I wanted to be like Bill. I hoped that
perhaps with hard work, by drawing down deep into myself and with a

little inspiration, I might one day come close to approaching his rhythmic way with words. Bill never lost that gift, and his last column for the *Post-Dispatch*, "The Time Has Come," written on the banks of the Meramec River, reminds us of what a magnificent gift it was.

Everyone knew that Bill was a beautiful writer, but over the years I also came to revere Bill as a reporter. His writing was so dazzling that you sometimes forgot from whence it came. His eye for detail, his description of a person or event, the remarkable quotes in his stories—all these were products of his reporting skills. He would be the first to say that they had been hewed and sharpened by his tutelage under Ray Lyle, the editor who made my life so miserable at the start of my career. Lyle was a powerful influence who drummed into all of us the sanctity of accuracy, attention to detail, the need to be specific in our writing and, above all, to vacuum up far more information than we could ever possibly use in a story, because we never knew on the spot what would ultimately be needed. Those were the fundamentals that guided us every day in our work, and no one ever took those lessons to heart more deeply than Bill.

Bill and I were friends for more than four decades, and as many times as we talked about writing, journalism, and public affairs, I had never actually witnessed Bill in action until after he went to Stanford. I began "visiting" his classes by phone from my office in New York or wherever I happened to be. Clustered around a speakerphone in his classroom, Bill and his students would pepper me with questions. Ostensibly, these chats were about reporting—the difficulty of knowing whether someone was telling the truth, the complexity of events, the nuts and bolts of the process itself. But in Bill's hands, these discussions became so much more—tales of human experience, moral values, the great lessons to be learned by building your craft one block at a time. Each forty-five-minute period moved along beautifully under Bill's guidance as gracefully as he shaped his writing. He invariably pulled information out of me that had long been buried. I understood for the first time the source of the rich detail that often showed up in his work; his low-key approach invariably got people to open up without their realizing it. After one particularly good session, I remember trying to reconstruct the arc of his interview to see what Bill had actually done, and then to file that knowledge away in hopes of using it in my own work. It was one more case of my learning from Bill, and, like that first lesson in Kansas City, that later lesson would stay with me forever.

James B. Steele
Philadelphia, Pa.

Acknowledgments

*T*his collection was made possible by the good work of Martha Shirk, William Woo's widow, and their three sons, Thomas, Bennett, and Peter Woo, who carefully went through the late author's computer files and retrieved a large collection of his writings. The family wishes to thank the many former students who supplied missing copies and encouraged the publication of this collection. The editor is grateful to Clair Willcox, John Brenner, and Jane Lago of University of Missouri Press for their care in supervising the preparation of the manuscript and to Nancy Pawlow, the Knight Chair assistant at the University of North Carolina, for her editorial help. Like any good writer, Professor Woo was constantly revising himself. Where multiple versions of a letter exist, the most recent was generally chosen. References to named students and transient classroom situations have been eliminated, and a few minor factual errors corrected. Otherwise, the material herein is presented as intended by the writer.

Letters from the Editor

Lessons on Journalism and Life

"I know that my retirement will make no difference in its cardinal principles, that it will always fight for progress and reform, never tolerate injustice or corruption, always fight demagogues of all parties, never belong to any party, always oppose privileged classes and public plunderers, never lack sympathy with the poor, always remain devoted to the public welfare, never be satisfied with merely printing news, always be drastically independent, never be afraid to attack wrong, whether by predatory plutocracy or predatory poverty."

Joseph Pulitzer, April 10, 1907

Introduction

*T*he career of William F. Woo tracked what many of our generation once considered the golden age of newspaper journalism. Looking back from a twenty-first-century perspective, it now seems more like an Indian summer, the brief return of warm and hazy days after the first killing frost and before the chill of winter.

It was at the start of such a season that I first met Bill. In the colorful September of 1966, that year's incoming class of Nieman fellows gathered in Harvard Yard for the orientation tour. The two of us quickly discovered a geographic bond. We had been educated at public universities in Kansas, and he had worked for the *Kansas City Times* when it was the morning *Kansas City Star.* That was the paper that had helped me learn to read when it was delivered to my childhood home in north-central Kansas.

Newspaper penetration, the ratio of circulation to households, peaked in the United States in 1922, but the industry was able to prosper for the remainder of the century through two strategies: consolidation and technical improvement. The first provided monopoly pricing power, and the second reduced the cost of production. Advertising salesmen learned to focus on average daily readership rather than circulation as the measure of success, and they promoted the fact that pass-along readership led 80 percent of adults to read a newspaper on an average day.

But high readership and financial success had a downside. Making money was too easy. In 1965, Osborn Elliott, the editor of *Newsweek* who would later become dean of the Columbia Graduate School of Journalism, commissioned a six-page special report on newspapers (November 29, 1965). It called the industry "fat—but smug, and, of all things, outdated." The cause was identified as old-guard ownership running on habit and feeling no need to invest in news and editorial improvement.

That malaise dissipated in the following decade. By 1971, the readership surveys had picked up a decline in newspaper reading that was so broad and so convincing that publishers started giving their readers more value in an effort to coax them back. Visiting my old outfit, the *Miami Herald,* while in Miami Beach for the 1972 presidential nominating conventions, I was both pleased and startled to see five reporters covering the beats—education, science, medicine, metropolitan government, civil rights—that only one or two of us had handled ten years earlier.

It was into this gathering atmosphere of reinvigoration that our Nieman class plunged when the precious year ended. Before Harvard, Bill Woo had been a feature writer for the *St. Louis Post-Dispatch.* Afterward, he was given the freedom to travel and dream up his own assignments on social and cultural trends.

He saw these projects as "essentially Harvard term papers turned into journalism," he told Daniel W. Pfaff, the author of *No Ordinary Joe: A Life of Joseph Pulitzer III* (University of Missouri Press, 2005). The topics included unemployment in the black community, America's housing problems, explicit sex in the cinema, life under the Soviets, and campus rebellion.

The work attracted attention and led to job offers from other papers. To keep Bill from jumping, the *Post-Dispatch* made him assistant editor of the editorial page. In 1973, he became editor of the storied page, which had been one of the first to criticize Senator Joseph R. McCarthy in the 1950s and to oppose the Vietnam War in the 1960s.

Bill enjoyed a close relationship with Pulitzer (although he was the third Joseph Pulitzer, he was called Joseph Pulitzer, Jr.). They were like father and son according to members of both families, and the older man gave him the freedom to grow in the job. Bill's personal history provided him with unusual empathy and the ability to reach across cultures. His parents had met at the University of Missouri's journalism school and eloped to Illinois to avoid Missouri's miscegenation laws. Bill was born in 1936 in Shanghai, where he spent the war years. Once he recalled watching from an upstairs porch as "wave after silver wave of American planes filled the sky with red and yellow parachutes." They were dropping supplies for westerners in Shanghai.

The Woos divorced after the war, and Bill was raised from the age of ten in Kansas City, Missouri, by his mother and elderly step-grandfather. As a mixed-race, bicultural child (a "twilight child," Bill called himself), he believed that he was destined to always be an observer. "I would venture that this twilight child can never truly be at home, that he finds himself forever outside looking in, even into the heart of his own families,"

Bill once wrote. "He has a perspective on himself and on the world that is beyond the experience of people born whole, either into a race or a culture."

He majored in English at the University of Kansas, and then reported for the *Times*. The *Post-Dispatch* hired him away five years later.

In 1986, in preparation for his eventual retirement, Joseph Pulitzer split the jobs of editor and publisher, which he then held, and made Bill the editor and Nicholas G. Penniman IV the publisher (the first time anyone outside the Pulitzer family held either title.) As editor, Bill continued writing opinion, using a Sunday column he called "A Reflection" to talk about issues of the day and relate them to everyday life, including his late-in-life experiences as father to three boys, Thomas, Bennett, and Peter.

"I wanted to look at the issues before America, but in a way that grew not out of what sources were saying, or inside stuff, but out of the experience of a life, which after all is the way that everyone ultimately looks at public matters," he wrote.

By the 1990s, the good times were fading for newspapers. They were a product of the Industrial Revolution, and they prospered because mass media were needed to sell the products of mass production. But as the industrial age morphed into the information age, both products and information became more specialized. Long before the Internet appeared, daily metropolitan newspapers were losing readers to more narrowly directed forms of media, including community papers. Advertisers found other ways to get their messages out.

The shift was particularly visible in retailing with boutiques of various descriptions crowding out the department stores. Shoppers fled the central cities for suburban malls where merchants could reach their customers with specialized publications. The ability of big-city publishers to raise prices in the face of declining readership reached its limit. So the publishers started cutting costs in an effort to hold on to their normal high profit margins. Staffs got smaller and even the size of the newspaper page shrank.

Joseph Pulitzer died in 1993, and his successor as chairman of the board, his half-brother, Michael Pulitzer, decided to "impose a more business-oriented leadership" in the newsroom, as the *New York Times* put it. Bill, a dedicated public-interest journalist, clung to the old values and opposed weakening the paper's progressive editorial voice and its watchdog role. The conflict led to his retirement and his move to Stanford in the fall of 1996, where he became the Lorry I. Lokey Visiting Professor in Journalism. He continued to write, but now in the form of weekly letters to his students. Each made a philosophical point about journalism and society and their delicate relationship in the good years in the last half of the twentieth century. "Even in my tenth year here, I still think of myself as a teacher on training wheels," he wrote students in his last letter a month before his death. "But as I hope is evident to you, I love being here—not wisely, I'm afraid, but too well."

Bill continued to uphold journalism's mission almost to the hour of his death on April 12, 2006. His last e-mail, composed the day before, urged his Stanford colleagues to increase the financial aid offer to a prospective student. His computer was still on when he died.

This volume has been formed from a selection of the letters, preserved as a way to remind the next generation of students and journalists of their craft's high purpose. The technology will change again. New ways of doing journalism—and new ways of paying for it—will be discovered. But the need to arm citizens "with the power which knowledge gives," as James Madison put it in the nineteenth century, will never change as long as democracy exists.

For the students and journalists of the twenty-first century, Bill Woo's platform is a reminder of the values worth preserving. Let it be their guide while they seek journalism's next season in the sun.

Philip Meyer
Chapel Hill, N.C.

Part I

What Business Are We In?

1

Never Be Satisfied with Merely Printing the News

A year or so before I left my position as editor of the *St. Louis Post-Dispatch* in 1996, the newspaper's top editors and managers interviewed a consultant—or "change agent," as some of them were being called—who might make us more creative. Change was the new thing in journalism. The air was full of "transactional change," "transformational change," the "dark night of the innovator," and so forth. After we'd finished interviewing the change agent, he asked what business we thought we were in. One by one, the chairman, assorted vice presidents, and managing editor gave the identical answer: We're in the information business.

When it came my turn, I disagreed. No, I said, we're in the news business. I said we were in the business of judgment, of discretion, of making informed decisions on what to publish. We were not in the business of spewing out undifferentiated information, like water from a garden hose.

The looks around the table said it all: Poor fellow, he just doesn't get it.

Not long thereafter, I recounted this to my old friend Philip Meyer, a professor of journalism at the University of North Carolina. When I told him the others declared we were in the information business, Phil replied, "Wrong answer." So I told him that I said we were in the news business. "Uh, oh," he said. "Also wrong answer."

So what is journalism's purpose? In my view, the purpose of journalism is not doing journalism—any more than the purpose of surgery is cutting patients open and sewing them back together again. The skill of the knife is important but only so far as it serves the larger purpose of surgery: restoring patients to health and productivity.

Similarly, the skill of journalists—their ability to report and edit well—is necessary for journalism to serve its purpose, which I consider a public trust. I once taught a course at the Graduate School of Journalism at Berkeley with Jay Harris, the former publisher of the *San Jose Mercury News,* devoted entirely to journalism's public trust. At the time, Jay had just resigned from the *Mercury News* in protest of the relentless bottom-line orientation of its parent company, Knight Ridder. He knew that people expect more from journalists than maximizing their employers' profits.

At my old newspaper, the *St. Louis Post-Dispatch,* we never conducted a focus group at which people told us they wanted to read about the plight of poor people, whose lives were often ones of squalor, affected by crime or a lack of education or multiple unplanned pregnancies. Quite the contrary. In fact, they told us nobody wanted to read about those things. And yet I knew that the public trust, at least as we defined it, required us to print such stories so our readers would have a better understanding of society and, hence, be better equipped to change it for the better.

American journalists came to embrace the idea that they had a public obligation for several reasons: The owners of important newspapers over many years came to see themselves as out to do more than get rich—though that was something they expected, as well. But when the requirement to spend money on the news meant smaller profits, they put the news—the public trust—first. The Sulzbergers at the *New York Times,* the Grahams at the *Washington Post,* the three generations of Joseph Pulitzers in St. Louis, the Binghams in Louisville, the Knights in Akron and Miami, the Poynter family in St. Petersburg, and many others, chose to be "philanthropists of news"—a wonderful phrase that I borrow from Jay.

The papers these owners created and managed over many decades were the incubators of the notion that journalism is about something more than the who, what, when, where—that journalists are involved in something essential to the concept of free men, free women, and a functioning and sustainable democracy.

We are in a period of technological, demographic, and attitudinal change, but to my mind, the greatest challenge in America's newsrooms relates to journalism's purpose. When the media lose sight of the public trust, they are letting the American people down. The disturbing truth is that we journalists have lost sight of our public trust; but it also has been deliberately obscured by the new ownership structure of the media and the incestuous relationship between the media and government.

Four recent books confront these developments in interesting and useful ways.

Nearly twenty-five hundred years ago, Sun Tzu, the Chinese military philosopher, addressed the importance of self-knowledge. If you know the enemy and know yourself, he wrote, you need not fear the result of a hundred battles. But if you know neither yourself nor the enemy, you will lose every time. When I was a young reporter in the 1950s, journalists knew themselves: They were in the newspaper business. Period. There was no confusion about it, and as for their enemies, they knew them chiefly by their absence. By the mid-1990s, when I left daily journalism, our competitors came in a bewildering array of print sources, broadcast media, and on-line sites—all hoping to capture advertising revenues that once were the domain of newspapers, all eager to replace newspapers as the preferred source of news, information, and advertising. No longer did we even know ourselves. What business were we in, anyway?

By the 1990s, the transformation of newspapers from privately owned companies to publicly traded ones had long been under way. Twenty years ago, in the first edition of his landmark book *The Media Monopoly,* Ben Bagdikian noted that fifty corporations controlled most of the country's newspapers, broadcasts, movies, and books. As he reports in *The New Media Monopoly,* that number has shrunk to five. In *The Problem of the Media,* Robert W. McChesney comprehensively documents the process by which the federal government has subsidized big media for nearly a century and a half. The roots of media monopolies were planted long ago, and by the 1990s they extended far underground.

As media consolidation has expanded, the media's fall from public grace has continued unabated. In 1972 a Gallup poll reported about 70 percent of people trusted the media. By 2000, Gallup found the figure had dropped to about 30 percent. What has changed? Government policies and the concentration of ownership have exacerbated the problems, but the loss in public confidence can also be attributed to a decline in journalistic quality, primarily through the subordination of news values to entertainment values. The public's waning confidence also reflects media executives' failure of nerve to pursue public issues, a course they rationalize on the grounds that their audiences are not interested in them. People, they say, want news you can use: stories about personal finance, personal health, and personal technology. Public issues do not qualify as news you can use, though what transpires in legislatures and city halls has more impact on readers and viewers than any number of articles on striking it rich in the Google auction or losing weight on low-carb diets.

The loss in public confidence is inextricably tied to the rise in educational levels, a strongly positive social trend that has the healthy side effect of encouraging the public to question what it reads and hears in the mass media. The loss is also related to the explosion in alternative sources of information, which allows people to make up their minds on the basis of a wider range of facts and opinion. Once people said they only knew what they read in the papers. It's unthinkable that anyone would seriously say such a thing nowadays.

Finally, journalism is scarcely the only public institution that has been challenged. Churches, universities, the law, corporations, government: All are shaken by doubts from without and within. Efforts to reform the media are unlikely to succeed without similar activities directed at other institutions central to American life.

For years scholars, activists, and journalists have discussed the effects of these changes on the country—"on democracy," they usually say. Not surprisingly, however, media companies have muted the response to the deeper issues of media concentration, as McChesney demonstrates through the belated news coverage of the Federal Communications Commission's efforts to relax media ownership regulations.

Bill Moyers describes the current situation in the media in his essay collection, *Moyers on America:*

> [D]espite plenty of lip service on every ritual occasion to freedom of the press, radio and TV, three powerful forces are undermining that very freedom. . . . The first of these is the centuries-old reluctance of governments—even elected governments—to operate in the sunshine of disclosure and criticism. The second is more subtle and more recent: the tendency of media giants, operating on big-business principles, to exalt commercial values at the expense of democratic value. . . . [The third is] the quasi-official partisan press ideologically linked to an authoritarian administration that in turn is the ally and agent of the most powerful financial interests in the world.

Moyers on America is a personable collection of wide-ranging speeches and commentaries. For the general reader it provides an excellent though brief description of the pressures that have been debasing the media—particularly, in his view, commercial television. Like Bagdikian and McChesney, Moyers worries about the effect on democracy. "What I find troubling today is democracy's inability to resolve some of the critical issues that face our nation," he writes. "These questions—all the more critical because of the growing disparities of wealth in this country—are almost entirely off the screen of public debate."

Bagdikian, a former dean of the Graduate School of Journalism at Berkeley, has long been respected as a perceptive herald of the consequences of concentration of media ownership. Through many editions of *The Media Monopoly*, he has laid out in fine detail how the obsession of owners to maximize profits has led them to ignore news that may interfere with their bottom lines. Now in *The New Media Monopoly*, Bagdikian has added a sharp and welcome political dimension. His first words to the reader are:

> In the years since 1980, the political spectrum of the United States has shifted radically to the far right. What was once the center has been pushed to the left, and what was the far right is now the center.

In *The Problem of the Media*, McChesney, a professor of communication at the University of Illinois, argues that the debasement of the media is the product of a historic collusion between government policy makers and a private media ownership driven by an insatiable desire for profits. He notes three duties of the press in a democracy: to be a watchdog, to ferret out truth, and to broadly present informed positions on important issues. On all three, he says, the media have failed:

> The problem stems directly from the system of profit-driven journalism in largely competitive markets that began to emerge over a century ago. This system was not "natural," but the consequence of a series of policies, most notably policies favoring monopoly and/or oligopoly . . . and commercialism in media.

McChesney finds a possible solution to the problem in what he calls "the uprising of 2003"—the unprecedented public opposition to the Federal Communications Commission's effort to further relax rules of media ownership. We have yet to learn whether the revolt will succeed.

McChesney tells an engrossing story of a dormant public aroused to indignation and action, but whether the opposition to the FCC's rules can be replicated is the question. For one thing, the public in this case had something specific to oppose as well as effective leadership within the FCC minority to carry the fight. But had the FCC not overreached, the country would still have been left with an indefensible concentration of media. Third, there has been a long history of government regulation over broadcasting, but nothing similar over the printed press, where the deleterious effects of concentration appear likely to remain.

Dan Gillmor, former technology columnist for the *San Jose Mercury News* and a friend who addresses my students each year, provides a different corrective in *We the Media*. Whereas McChesney envisions a frontal assault on the government–private ownership cartel, Gillmor sees a million holes drilled through it by "citizen journalists."

Gillmor looks forward to "journalism's transformation from a twentieth-century mass-media structure to something profoundly more grassroots and democratic," a transformation made possible through new technologies like blogs, SMS (short message services), mail lists, the Wiki phenomenon, mobile phones with cameras, Internet broadcasting, peer-to-peer file sharing, and RSS (Rich Site Summary, also known as Real Simple Syndication). These applications are used by citizen journalists around the world; indeed, it was through SMS that Chinese reporters first learned of the SARS epidemic.

Gillmor foresees a fundamental shift in news from a lecture by the media to a conversation among professional journalists, citizen journalists, and others with something to add to the discussion:

> The lines will blur between producers and consumers, changing the role of both in ways we're only beginning to grasp now. The communication network itself will be a medium for everyone's voice, not just the few who can afford to buy multi-million-dollar printing presses, launch satellites or win the government's approval to squat on the public's airwaves.
>
> Accuracy and fairness no doubt will take some buffeting in the process. I do not minimize the effects of this turbulence. Even so, the contribution of more voices, more opinions, and more facts will surely enrich the discussion of important issues.

Gillmor's vision of American society comes closest to my own, which is that democracy is a means, not an end or objective. Personal liberty or freedom is the end, and democracy is the way that we Americans have chosen to try to achieve it.

Hence, the debasement of the media can be likened to the failure of an automobile's engine. It is serious, perhaps catastrophic. Fortunately, we can still walk, though that effort may not be for everyone.

We the Media shows how citizens and journalists alike can contribute truth, accurate information, and provocative opinion without the need for what is controlled by the government–private ownership cartel. There are ways to address that cartel, though it would take another essay to describe them. In the meantime, if we cannot ride, then let us walk.

Republished in the Cardinal Inquirer *with permission of* UUWorld, *the magazine of the Unitarian Universalist Association. This review appeared in the November/December 2004 issue.*

2

My Old Secondhand Sweater

I suspect none of you paid any attention to the old secondhand tan sweater I wore to class Wednesday. There's really no reason to have given it a second look. There are millions like it. Yet the old thing means more to me than just about anything else I own. The sweater belonged to Joseph Pulitzer, my boss. When he died, his widow gave it to me.

I've warned you to be careful of writing commentary that goes no further than your own experiences. It may gall us, but the truth is, readers respond more strongly to stories that either touch them or relate to some greater purpose or cause than to those that merely lay out for the world what interesting lives we think we have.

So what can I say about this sweater that would be relevant to what we are about together, which is exploring journalism and how to write it in a way that is faithful to its best values? Let me begin by telling you about Joe Pulitzer.

He was the grandson and namesake of that half-blind, half-mad genius who changed the face and course of journalism. The first Joseph Pulitzer founded the *St. Louis Post-Dispatch*, owned the *New York World*, endowed the school of journalism at Columbia University, and gave the money for the Pulitzer Prizes. He invented investigative reporting, made crusades a part of journalism, and wrote the business model that sustained newspapers for more than a century.

Not much was expected of his son, the second Joseph Pulitzer. The founder kept him in St. Louis and sent another son to New York, where the action was. But the *World* languished and eventually was sold, while in St. Louis the second Joseph Pulitzer was turning the *Post-Dispatch* into the most admired paper of its day. By the time he died in 1955, the *Post-Dispatch* had won five Pulitzer Prizes for meritorious public service—

more than any other paper to the end of the twentieth century. (The *New York Times* received its fifth in 2004.)

The second Joseph Pulitzer's son, also named Joseph, had a rough beginning as a newspaper publisher. He was devastated by the death of his father, whom he so admired that until the day he died he referred to himself not as Joseph Pulitzer III but as J. P. Jr. in memos to his staff. He used Junior in his formal business dealings. A psychologist could make something of that. Among friends, he wanted to be called Joe.

His father drank whiskey and went duck hunting with his editors. Sometimes there were fistfights. Joe never had such experiences. At Harvard, he was trained as an art historian. As an undergraduate, he bought his first Expressionist painting, Modigliani's "Elvira Resting at a Table." Eventually, he amassed one of the world's great art collections. If you had a drink in his pool house, you sat beneath Monet's water lilies.

Joe was refined, aristocratic, and terribly shy. He always took the stairs—fitness, he said, but I believed it was for fear of running into his staff and having to make conversation. Yet, as a young naval officer, he had fought on the ground at Iwo Jima, in one of history's bloodiest battles.

When his father died in 1955, J. P. Jr. took over the paper, as editor and publisher. Some people called him a fop, or worse. What did he know about the rough and tumble of journalism? But in his veins ran the blood of the first Joseph Pulitzer. He understood the purpose of journalism and its potential for greatness.

He was ill at ease with reporters and editors, but he was eloquent in talking about their mission. As he told an audience at Columbia University, "a newspaper that has no substance at its core is taking a frivolous view of its place in society; and it may be risking its future."

On his watch were momentous changes in journalism: the full effect of television, the first stirrings of on-line information, the hemorrhage in circulation, the awful drop in public confidence, and the revolution in newspaper financing. As chairman, he saw the fortunes of his company placed in the hands of Wall Street.

Now as all this was going on, and for years utterly unknown to J. P. Jr., I was making my way across the landscape of what turned out to be a career. I came to his attention after a Nieman Fellowship at Harvard, for which he always maintained a soft spot. At the time, I was trying to do a new kind of long take-out series for the *Post-Dispatch*—explanatory journalism as it was later called.

In the late 1960s, the *New York Times* and *Newsweek* simultaneously offered me jobs. J. P. Jr. sent a note saying, Don't do anything stupid. With that word came more money and an opportunity to do work that might help our readers better understand the world—from their own city to far beyond the horizons. So I stayed, and as time passed he gave me new responsibilities.

We must have made an odd couple: the elegant, cultured man with journalism's most honored pedigree and the Chinese-American street reporter from Kansas City, educated at a state university and for years nearly dead broke. What connected us, I think, was a mutual conviction that there was more to journalism than today's paper, no matter how good it might be. There was a public purpose; there was a social mission; there was, by god, something we ought to do every day to earn our keep under the First Amendment. Our job was to figure that out.

Every week we lunched, with first drinks and then conversation. Every week we talked about the Pulitzer Platform. What did it mean to "never lack sympathy with the poor"? What coverage, what editorial position, reflected that command? How could we "always be drastically indepen- dent" when advertisers, politicians, social elites, and others assumed they had the press in their pockets? Had we kept the faith lately?

In a way, he was the father I never had. He pounded the table, roared in anger at me, had faith in me, supported me against all enemies, no matter how powerful. When the chairman of the telephone company (later the mega-giant SBC) was furious over something I put in the pa- per, J. P. Jr. said to hell with him and in so doing cost the paper the util- ity's advertising for many years.

He made me the first editor of the *St. Louis Post-Dispatch* whose name was not Joseph Pulitzer, and I am so proud of that. In so doing, he passed over his own family, and I wonder now what that meant for the future. I have my ideas, but that's a story for another time. He trained me as an editor, just as back in Kansas City Mr. Lyle had trained me as a reporter.

And then he died. The cancer hung around on the margins and then began its inexorable advance. In May 1993, I went to Croatia to talk about ethics but more fundamentally, I went because there was action there. A war was still sputtering along, and all my life I have wanted to be "there," as every reporter who wants his story on the front page wants to be there. His wife, Emily, called me in Zagreb and said to get home on the next plane.

The last time I saw J. P. Jr., he was dying. I had a few minutes with him, and I told him that I had brought back some good stories for the paper. It probably sounds silly, but in that moment I wanted him to know I thought of him always as the man who ran the *Post-Dispatch*. But what he said was, "I'm so pleased for you," in a voice I had to strain to hear; and those were the last words he spoke to me.

At his funeral, I was among those who said a few things. From the balcony three singers gave us the lovely, perfect farewell from the first act of Mozart's "Cosi Fan Tutte"—*soave sia il vento:* "Gentle be the breeze, calm be the waves . . ."

So that is the story of the sweater and what it means to me. Not a month goes by without a visit from J. P. Jr. in the still hours after midnight. He belongs to what I call my Repertory Company of the Dead— a half dozen or so people, all gone now, who meant so much to me and who return again and again in my dreams.

Every now and then, I wear that old sweater in remembrance of lessons I need still to practice. I try every day still to live up to ideals he taught me—and those that he himself tried to achieve, ultimately in vain, of course. It would not have been a life for him, nor for me, had it been otherwise.

3

A Personal Life and an Occupation

*H*ave you read *Dandelion Wine,* Ray Bradbury's book about a boy's magical summer in a simpler time, many years ago? Some of you have, I'm sure.

You may remember how the boy goes to pick dandelions for the wine his grandfather makes. When the flowers have been pressed and the purest rainwater they can find has been added, they store the bottles in the cellar, one for every day of the summer. Months later, when the days are cold and dark, a sip of dandelion wine brings back the warm golden glow of another season.

I had a day this week that I wish I could bottle like Ray Bradbury's dandelion wine. It was an Indian summer day, bright and warm with a beautiful blue sky. Even when I was young, those were bittersweet days.

After lunch Monday, I drove north into Marin County, to a place just beyond Point Reyes. I was going to talk with the staff of ACFNewsource, which provides programs for *The Osgood File* and other radio shows. They wanted to discuss how journalists deal with the tension between their work and their efforts to be men and women fully engaged with life.

Those tensions, between a personal life and an occupation, exist to some extent among all people. But journalists, as you are coming to know, are different. My friend Bob Steele at the Poynter Institute writes, "No other individuals have the primary and constitutionally protected role of regularly informing and educating the public in a meaningful way on significant issues." How much are we restrained by that?

The music all day was heavenly. Murray Perahia chased me across the Golden Gate Bridge with the one of Mozart's B flat major piano concertos, written when he was a lot younger than any of you. There were white sails in the bay, and to the left the Pacific stretched westward toward China.

Later, west of U.S. 101, the road wound through a dark grove of redwoods, and then, after a few turns, it was back into bright sunlight. It went past a wonderfully restored little red schoolhouse built in the 1870s. The music was Beethoven's, the "Moonlight Sonata."

The retreat was at the Marconi Center, which is run by the state parks and was the place the great inventor tried to develop telegraph signals strong enough to cross the Pacific. There were about ten ACFNewsource people there, all of them thoughtful and friendly. With the sun still high in the sky, we sat on the porch and talked about journalists and their conflicts when they participate as social and political beings.

We discussed bringing politics into a news organization. What's the difference between wearing a button for a candidate and putting a campaign poster in your cubicle? What's the difference between asking colleagues to sign a petition and asking for time to hold a rally in the newsroom?

In the famous Tinker case, in which some high-school students in Des Moines, Iowa, were sent home for wearing armbands to protest the Vietnam War, the Supreme Court said the Bill of Rights does not stop at the schoolhouse door. But what about the newsroom door? What restraints or prohibitions against speech or assembly may news organizations reasonably apply?

You may recall another famous case involving a war protestor named Robert Cohen who wore a jacket with the words "F*** the Draft" on it. He was arrested and convicted of obscenity, but the Supreme Court held that those words were a political statement and hence protected. But, I asked the ACF people, what if Robert Cohen had worn that jacket to his grandmother's house for Sunday dinner? Would she have to seat him at the table?

No. The First Amendment would not be violated had she said, "Young man, take that jacket off if you want to eat in my house." So it is in newsrooms. The right to free speech and the unfettered practice of free speech are not the same. In a way, we are all Robert Cohen at Sunday dinner, with legal rights that may have to yield to practical, everyday restrictions on their expression.

I told the group about Lou Dobbs, the CNN financial reporter, and how in the early 1990s, the *Wall Street Journal* had reported on his promotional work for Shearson Lehman Brothers and Payne Webber. Lou Dobbs was offended that his ethics had been called into question. It was a perfectly legitimate way to make some extra money. The videos he had made for these outfits were meant only for in-house training, he said. Nonetheless, after some dithering, CNN reprimanded him.

But now a bright young man named Andrew interjected to say that Lou Dobbs also made subjective judgments in his reports on financial issues. Dobbs justified these, he said, by asserting that his long experience qualified him to ignore what other journalists might think of as objectivity or neutrality. It brought value to his reports on CNN. So where did I stand on that?

This increasingly is a difficult issue for journalists. Often, they are the most informed people around on particular subjects or issues. A reporter who has covered local government for twenty years probably knows more about City Hall than anyone else. Yet the conventions of our profession require that to be "objective," the reporter must seek out comments from sources, and the sources may be wholly ignorant of the issues. Instead of the most informed perspective, readers get the least informed. Why criticize Lou Dobbs?

The easy answers to such questions are usually facile. Competing values are in play. On one side, there is the value of the reporter's expertise. On the other, there's the news organization's credibility, which may suffer if its reporters are allowed to mingle opinions with their news presentations.

How to exploit the expertise and at the same time maintain credibility? The conventional forms of journalism may not work here. We can begin by looking at alternative methods of doing stories that harm neither value. Usually, with a lot of thinking, you can find a way.

But if you cannot, then I would say that credibility is the key value. CNN's credibility over the long term prevails over whatever authority Lou Dobbs can bring to a particular story. Finding expertise elsewhere is usually a lot easier than resuscitating credibility.

That's the way the conversation went. When the sun went behind the trees and it got chilly, we repaired indoors and kept talking. About 5:30, two and a half hours after we'd begun, I took my leave.

The light was fading over the shallow waters of Tomales Bay as I drove south. Centuries ago, this was where the Miwoks lived and harvested oysters. Then came Sir Francis Drake and later the Russian fur traders, all before what we know now as Californians settled there.

As it grew dark, I heard a Haydn Mass with a Kyrie so lively and irresistible that somewhere angels boogied. It made me think again of creativity in the service of a great idea. That's an energy that each of us as journalists can summon. Before me, the yellow reflector dots lighted up the road as if it were an airport runway.

But when I got home, things were tense. Peter had been a handful all evening, defiant about homework. From his room came chords from a guitar. Martha, tired and stressed, was staring into her computer. Those of you who become parents will know this scene.

The best thing I could do was to stay out of the way. So I went back downstairs and made a stiff Scotch and soda, and then I grilled some small lamb chops out on the deck. For once, I had the sense not to talk about the great day I'd had.

4
A Journalist's Thanksgiving

This letter comes to you early in Thanksgiving week. On the day before Thanksgiving, if tradition holds, the *Wall Street Journal* will publish an editorial that runs every year.

It will contain a passage written in 1620 by Nathaniel Morton, the historian of the Plymouth Colony. Since 1961, the *Journal* has run it every Wednesday before Thanksgiving. Morton's observance of the voyage of the *Mayflower* and the experience of the pilgrims' first year in the New World begins like this:

> So they left that goodly and pleasant city of Leyden, which had been their resting-place for above eleven years, but they knew that they were pilgrims and strangers here below, and looked not much on these things, but lifted up their eyes to Heaven . . .

It's the *Journal*'s way of reflecting on the day and giving thanks for it. In similar fashion, each year, I send my students what I've come to think of as a Journalist's Thanksgiving. Every time, as with the one you're reading, the piece goes through a little revision, but the sentiment is always the same.

This year, our family will be observing Thanksgiving at the home of some friends. The boys will all be with us, and for that I am not only thankful but happy. I expect that the moment will come when one by one, going around the table, we'll all talk about something we are thankful for. That's a tradition in many American families, and yet I am always a little uncomfortable with it.

For one thing, the parts of your life for which you give thanks often are intensely private, while some are so obvious as to make anything said about them sound trite. When your thanks go further afield, they can be hard to explain in a minute or two; and anyway other people may not be interested.

I have in mind, for example, an editor I met one summer in the northern Thailand city of Chiang Mai. I may have mentioned him to you. I do not know how I would talk about him at a Thanksgiving dinner.

I had gone to Chiang Mai to give a speech on press freedom, and beforehand there was a lunch with local journalists. Among them was this editor named Amnat Khunyosying. His paper, *Pak Nua Raiwan,* was highly critical of local officials and he was warned to lay off. Amnat kept digging at the truth and one day as he was getting into his pickup truck, someone pulled up alongside, pushed a 9-mm pistol through the window, and opened fire, severely wounding him.

The army is never far from Thai politics, and Amnat's assailants turned out to be four soldiers. They were quickly apprehended, but the local prosecutor was afraid to bring charges, because of where that might lead. If it hadn't been for the insistence of other local journalists, he might have let the case drop. On the day we had lunch, the police told Amnat that a couple of out-of-town trigger men had been spotted in Chiang Mai. Watch your back, the cops said.

But there at the lunch, Amnat was holding forth against official corruption as if it were the easiest thing in the world to talk about. The motto of his paper, by the way, is "Every drop of ink builds the future, builds the truth." In that moment, I was truly thankful for him and for the brave men and women around the world whose daily struggles are a testament to the power of an idea, namely, that the freedom to think and to write and to speak is the dividing line between liberty and slavery.

The Thai journalists at the table that day had many stories to tell of physical and economic intimidation. They asked if American journalists faced similar threats, and I had to say that while our work is not always easy, it rarely is what anyone would call dangerous—at least the work we do in the United States. They seemed to think that our First Amendment protected us from threats and assassination attempts.

It does no such thing, of course, though in other ways its protections are incalculable. Exactly what the First Amendment means has been subject to interpretation over the years. But its unique blessing has been to stand as a guarantee that the power of government must not be used to suppress the ability of the people to speak or write what is on their minds or in their hearts. I believe this is what we as journalists have most to be thankful for, today and always.

Now and then you see surveys showing that many Americans are unsympathetic with the First Amendment. At times, we the press have done our best to make it even less popular. Many of us seem to think that the amendment was written for the press, rather than for the people, and that it confers upon us special privileges or rights that are not given to others.

I think that assumption is part of the problem of the media's arrogance, about which people understandably complain. There is almost no phrase used by journalists that I dislike more than "the public's right to know," for it so often justifies not courage and independence but excess, intrusion, and abuse.

As poll after poll shows, our business falls ever more sharply from the public's grace, and the press has struggled to repair the damage. You hear editors talk about "reconnecting with our communities." That's a worthy objective, but it also contains a danger of associating ourselves with orthodoxy and the status quo.

The American Society of Newspaper Editors a few years ago set up something called the Journalism Values Institute. Its purpose was to rededicate journalists to the "core values" of our profession, which presumably are better than ordinary everyday values. The JVI put out a handbook that recommended that news stories focus not only on the good and the bad but also on the "profoundly ordinary." The trouble is, too much of our journalism celebrates the profoundly ordinary, which is another way of saying orthodoxy.

So you can imagine how thrilled I was to listen to a speech by the novelist Salman Rushdie at the last ASNE convention I attended as an editor. That was in 1996, and Rushdie, as you may remember, had been living under threat of death from Iran. His novel *Satanic Verses* was said to be disrespectful to Islam. Rushdie spoke about "respect," and a few lines from his speech are my Thanksgiving gift to you.

Rushdie noted that "Fine as the word sounds, truth is all too often unpalatable, awkward, unorthodox. The armies of received ideas are marshaled against it."

He went on to observe that we live in a censorious age, and one of the most prominent weapons of censorship is a new concept of respect. Once respect meant consideration and serious attention. Now respect means agreement, and any dissent from someone's position—indeed any inquiry into it—is regarded as disrespect. Disagree with people and they say you've dissed them. Editors know that there is almost no story that someone will not find "disrespectful."

"I want to suggest to you," said Rushdie (and these are the words that I would like to say at a Thanksgiving table), "that citizens of free societies, democracies, do not preserve their freedom by pussyfooting around their fellow citizens' opinions, even their most cherished beliefs. . . . A free society is not a calm and eventless place—that is the kind of static, dead society dictators try to create. Free societies are dynamic, noisy, turbulent, and full of radical disagreements . . .

"It is the disrespect of journalists—for power, for orthodoxy, for party lines, for ideologies, for vanity, for arrogance, for folly, for pretension, for corruption, for stupidity—that I would like to celebrate this morning, and that I urge you all, in freedom's name, to preserve."

In some news organizations today, my students, a curious kind of courage prevails. It is the courage to be popular, the courage to recklessly reflect the conventional view, the courage to fearlessly exalt the profoundly ordinary. Salman Rushdie was talking about a different kind of courage, and it is the one I commend to you.

That courage requires disrespect, and it results in the relentless search for truth, no matter what the consequences; for without truth, men and women cannot really be free—for without truth no democracy can endure. I think my friend Amnat in Chiang Mai would understand. He was willing to take terrible risks for it, and on this Thanksgiving Day I shall be thinking about him—and about you, also.

5

Our Journalism and Our Humanity

Since before the days of Ernest Hemingway, every new reporter at the *Kansas City Star* has been given a copy of the paper's stylebook that begins with what the *Star* describes as a "20-word guide to good writing." Upon Hemingway, it made a lasting impression. Years later as a world famous author, he is said to have come into the *Star* newsroom, quoting from the stylebook.

"Those were the best rules I ever learned for the business of writing," he told an interviewer. "I've never forgotten them. No man with any talent, who feels and writes truly about the thing he is trying to say, can fail to write well, if he abides by them."

My copy of the stylebook is discolored by age and spotted by the spilling of liquids that today are prohibited in newsrooms everywhere. But there on page three, under GENERAL STYLE are the words that Hemingway and generations of young *Star* reporters were taught by:

> Use short sentences. Use short first paragraphs. Use vigorous English, not forgetting to strive for smoothness. Be positive, not negative.

All the rules in the world, of course, will not guarantee that one will become a good writer, much less one of the great ones in American literature. Hemingway himself paid a separate tribute to something as important as rules, and that was the instruction he received at the *Star.* In 1958, he told the *Paris Review:*

> On the Star, you were forced to learn to write a simple declarative sentence. That's useful to anyone.

Useful to anyone and the foundation of great literature: In the beginning God created the heavens and the earth. Call me Ishmael. It was a bright cold day in April, and the clocks were striking thirteen. In a hole in the ground there lived a hobbit.

As you can see, I am drifting, or pulled perhaps by the magnetic force of the simple declarative sentence. So back to the twenty-word guide to good writing; back to commentary. Note how it ends: *Be positive, not negative.* For years I puzzled over these four words. How were they pertinent to the journalist whose mission was to illuminate reality, unpleasant and unwelcome as it might be?

The other day I asked you to read an op-ed contribution to the *Arizona Republic* from a man who lives in White Mountain Lake, which Google tells me is about 130 miles northeast of Phoenix. It started with his views on traffic cameras and ended with a proposal to fine speeders one thousand dollars with possible jail sentences. It took a swipe at gas prices, six-tire pickups, the failure of self-governance, and, of course, taxes.

I didn't care much for the piece but I hadn't got my arms around what was really nettling me about it until one of you said, this was an angry man. Suddenly, things clicked. Set in the context of speeders, his article projected a deep discontent with the way the world, or his piece of it, was going. Who was the author? What motivated him? We could only guess—if we cared to make the effort.

Anger, like other emotions, is a legitimate and often effective element of commentary writing, but it rarely works if that is all there is to it. As a tone, it is one-dimensional.

We also read an odd op-ed from the *Los Angeles Times* about Martin Luther King's "other woman." I found several problems with the piece—content, timing, and taste among them. But surely there was also a problem of tone. For from start to finish, this was a piece that exuded slyness, smugness, and hypocrisy.

Unfocused anger, slyness, smug self-satisfaction. These are what the *Star* stylebook warned of when it counseled reporters to be positive, not negative. The old *Star* editors understood that readers are naturally engaged by a positive tone. What was it the Spoken Word artist said on that Mos Def poetry video? Be assertive. Have confidence in what you say.

Over time, I have come to believe that what the stylebook meant above all is that the issue of being positive or negative is often settled by tone. We know that to be true in our daily lives.

The whiner, the complainer, the know-it-all, the one with the strident voice—all of them may have important things to say. But we're likely to find their tone so irritating that we tune them out. Turning readers off is not our objective.

In commentary, there's a time for sarcasm, but it's not all the time. Similarly, there's a time for gravity or lightheartedness but do it too often and the readers will evaporate. And always remember, we're writing for them. Long ago, I learned a painful and embarrassing lesson about tone and timing. Perhaps there's something in it for you to think about.

It took place back in Jimmy Carter's administration. Iranians had seized the U.S. embassy in Tehran and were holding fifty-three Americans hostage. Negotiations were long and fruitless. Then in April 1980, some six months after the hostages had been taken, Carter launched a bold rescue mission.

That night, as America slept, the rescue had come to grief two hundred miles south of Tehran at a place the military called Desert One. Helicopters, launched from aircraft carriers, were to land Rangers at the embassy. Once freed, the hostages would be ferried to Desert One, where C-130s would fly them out.

The trouble was, everything had gone wrong. A sandstorm forced the helicopters down at Desert One before they got to Tehran. A helicopter and a C-130 collided, sending up a giant fireball and killing five of the rescue party.

Back in Washington, the White House began calling the press corps for a pre-dawn briefing. I was asleep in my apartment in the Adams-Morgan neighborhood in Washington when I got the call from our bureau around 4 a.m. I was in Washington, writing editorials and columns, on leave from my regular job as editorial page editor.

Everyone scrambled, and by first light stories were being filed. In those days, the *Post-Dispatch* came out in the afternoon, so I had until 8 a.m. Washington time to get an editorial into the paper. I made the deadline with time to spare. It was the best editorial I had ever written.

This was a coldly analytical piece, as sharp as an icicle, as pitiless as a banker's smile. From concept to execution, the rescue was deeply flawed, I wrote with barely controlled indignation. Strategically miscarried. Shortsighted. Wrong equipment. Hopeless. Five deaths were bad, but taken to completion, it would have been worse. My sources in the defense think tanks said so.

I filed the piece and sat back, waiting for the congratulatory call from a grateful office in St. Louis. Shortly after the first edition went to press, the telephone rang.

It was my deputy, who was running the page while I was away. What he said was that Joseph Pulitzer, the chairman, had personally ordered my editorial removed from the paper. I was crushed. Nothing like this had ever happened to me. But Joe Pulitzer was right.

Weeks later, when I was back in St. Louis for a visit, he and I had lunch. We started, as we always did, with drinks, and after the second Scotch he said he was sorry to have had to kill my editorial. He knew I had worked hard on it.

But then he said that there is a time for analysis and a time for cold logic, a time for the icicle. That time, however, is not the moment when the country is in shock, when people are stunned by the deaths of Americans on a distant errand of rescue.

Now was the time for something other than a frigid, crystalline piece of prose. Now was the time for quiet, like the soft footfall of people at a funeral. It was time for sadness and respect for men who had undertaken something dangerous for a good cause and had failed. There would be an occasion for all the logic and the blame and the political fallout, but that was later.

And of course that was the right way to look upon it. We get so carried away by what we imagine to be our brilliance that we forget to bring our journalism in line with our humanity. We may think that our words arise from celestial music when in fact they come from our being tone deaf to the world.

I know now the Desert One editorial was an exercise in self-gratification, which is driven by negative ambitions, not positive ones. At an awful time when the paper should have been helping its readers, I wanted everyone to see how smart I was. The tone I selected was one of intellectual certainty. I had forgotten the difference between writing for yourself and for the people who read you, and I have tried very hard ever since never to confuse the two.

6

The Great Purpose

A few months ago, I got an e-mail from a friend of mine named Peter, saying that his on-line publication was going out of business. This wasn't another dot-com skyrocket fizzling out. Peter never had a stock option in his life, never got within a million miles of an IPO. This wasn't the *New Economy* shutting down. It was his body. My friend Peter is a quadriplegic.

It is difficult to make those things attached to his hands work the computer, and after many years, it became too much. As he explained, with what seemed a little embarrassment, "as you know, my body barely works (even if my mind does). Glad to be out from under all that—but have some 'quitters' remorse' as I think of things I wish I'd said or want to say (particularly with this weird, prolonged election). Like the old dog at the firehouse, I still hear the bell and want to go. I expect I'll keep on writing. Op-eds? A column? Letters-To-The-Editor? Maybe just letters?"

Peter used to be one of my editorial writers on the *Post-Dispatch*. He was an Iowa boy, the son of the local Ford dealer, who went to the state university. He had that sense of the people who come out of the rhythms of farms and the small towns that we city-bred journalists often don't have.

Somewhere along the way, he picked up a curiosity about the world and an idealism that never wavered. Early in our friendship, when we were still both reporters, I ran into him in Moscow, of all places. I was writing; he was on a leave of absence, traveling the world with some leftish group that was trying to find out how to make peace work.

Later we both became editorial writers, and we had wonderful, wacky times. Once the newspaper union went on strike and we were all out of work. Peter and I and some others started a strike newspaper. Of course, we couldn't afford a wire service. Peter, who was a gadgeteer and a tinkerer, figured out how to steal the UPI stories from the satellite, and we hooked up a printer to this contraption he'd whipped out. We called it our Galactic News Bureau, news from the heavens, and I'll never forget the moment we turned it on. The printer made some noise and everybody cheered. Then our first story started chattering out. It was . . . the European soccer results, in Spanish!

Peter was a lovely editorial writer but he was an even better editor. Sometimes I would get pieces from the staff that defeated me, and I'd turn them over to Peter. He had this intuitive sense of the writer's intent, and with a few strokes he'd make the piece right, preserving the journalist's pride and ownership.

He was always under pressure at home for money, and finally he took a job at the University of Illinois, because we couldn't pay him what he needed and what he was worth. Life went well for him for awhile, and then one day, out of the terrible blue, he had a stroke so bad that it left him barely able to speak and for all purposes paralyzed. He was still a young man, in his forties. It took years for him to be able even to move a hand, up or down. But once he could do that, he got someone to rig up a stylus that was taped to his wrist, and thus, slowly, painfully, he began to write again. Once again, he would be a journalist.

But what kind of journalist is tied to a wheelchair and a bed? Unable to do interviews, unable even to call anyone. He could take notes but even that was unbearably slow. Hand up, an inch to the right, hand down: the letter "t." Now hand back up, two more inches right and back down again: the letter "o." He has tapped out the word "to." Now hand up again. What kind of a journalist would work that way? Well, Peter would. For that was the only way there was to do it.

But where would he get information? Television—the network news, what public affairs programming he could find and that great underappreciated resource, C-SPAN, which trains its cameras on Congress and hearings and press conferences and important speeches and just lets the cameras roll. Now he had a way to keep up with the world, and he had the journalistic form to illuminate and make sense of it. It was the editorial.

So Peter started a little paper called "TV and Politics Watch." He got it out once a month, or as close to that as he could, and for a year's worth of these, he asked for twenty-five dollars. You've heard of the Lonely Pamphleteer. Peter gave the phrase a whole new meaning. Sometimes his paper came in the mail. Sometimes by e-mail. Some months it didn't come at all.

His role model was I. F. Stone, the last of the muckrakers. Izzy Stone worked with paper. He read the texts of congressional hearings and government reports. He read the texts of press conferences. He read books and everything else he could get his hands on. He didn't go to the scene or conduct interviews. He worked from documents, which he read more thoroughly than anyone else. He had a little paper called "I. F. Stone's Weekly." And back in the 1960s and 1970s, if you wanted to understand what was going on in the dim corners of government or how high and mighty politicians were getting away with lying in their teeth, you had to read Izzy Stone.

There's an important investigative reporting award named after I. F. Stone. Very few people have ever heard of my friend Peter and nothing's likely to be named for him. But he worked as hard as any journalist who has ever lived, and for the purpose that all editorialists—yourselves included, I hope—serve, namely, to offer a point of view about the world and its people and to help readers understand them and come to judgment.

Here's the last editorial he wrote in his little paper, before he folded it. It comes, of course from watching C-SPAN. It's 130 words long, which isn't much, of course, unless you're writing it one laborious letter after another, hand up, hand down.

> SNL in the House
> The timing was right out of TV's "Saturday Night Live." But the comedy was real, though unintended.
> There on the House floor was Jim Trafficante, the Republicans' favorite Democrat, under scrutiny by the Justice Department, and just by coincidence finding fault with Democratic Attorney General Janet Reno, accusing her of "treason."
> Then a Republican lawmaker, after denouncing the media for being "biased" toward Vice President Gore, extolled the importance of the press to democracy, the importance of openness.
> This was followed by a message from the Senate requesting a conference with the House on the CIA budget bill—the amount of which is secret from the press and the public.
> The juxtaposition was humorous—as long as one doesn't think too hard what it says about American democracy.

I think of my friend often, but particularly whenever my own writing seems burdensome, whenever looking up a fact, or checking a citation, or reading one more source, when all these seem more trouble than I should bear. Peter never lost faith with the great purpose of journalism, which so often I overlook but which, in my better moments, I try to pass on to you, in our classes, in letters such as these. Good opinion matters. Good perspective matters. Doing the rigorous work to extract or uncover the facts, so as to be able to tell what happened and not what might have happened or should have happened matters most of all.

When I think of Peter a few lines from a play by Archibald MacLeish come to mind. They were among his favorites. The lines come from MacLeish's play "J.B.," which is a modern dramatization of the Book of Job, that good man of the Bible who suffered so terribly and seemingly pointlessly but who never cursed his god for it. Job endured and so has Peter.

The lines go like this:

> Take the even, take the odd,
> I would not sleep here if I could
> Except for the little green leaves in the wood
> And the wind on the water.

Those small things, of course, the little green leaves in the wood and the wind on the water, are only memories for Peter now. I wonder what it would be like never to see them again. He managed, though, and he moved on. What next for him? Op-eds? Columns? Letters to the editor? Maybe just letters? Like that old firehouse dog, he still hears the bell and wants to go. Never feel sorry for a man like that. Feel sorry for those who never hear the bell and who never go.

7

Who Owns a Newspaper?

Who owns a newspaper? Who owns the *Washington Post*? The *San Jose Mercury News*? The *St. Louis Post-Dispatch*? The *Palo Alto Daily News*, the *Grass Valley Union*? Who owns any newspaper? The answer is not as simple as you might think.

The question of newspapers and their owners has been on my mind recently. As I told you, Jay Harris, the former publisher of the *San Jose Mercury News*, and I are teaching a course at Berkeley called The Public Trust.

It's our premise that somewhere in the last thirty years or so, certainly since Al Neuharth took Gannett public in the 1960s, an evolutionary change of then unimaginable proportions took place in the development of America's newspapers. That change turned upside down what we nominally think of as ownership.

What had been an intensely private industry, largely made up of family-owned newspapers or groups, suddenly and with a breathtaking sweep became a publicly owned industry. Where once these companies were owned by men and women with a focus on news and news values— a focus, if you will, on the public service mission of their family companies—suddenly they became owned by investors with little or no interest in journalism or its public responsibilities.

We've talked about this in our class. Remember how I told you that at the Boston Media Conference put on by stock analysts last December, the executives of Gannett, the nation's largest chain of newspapers, never mentioned the word "journalism" even once?

What we haven't talked about, though, is the possibility that a newspaper may have more than one owner or group of owners. I myself hadn't thought much about this until one day in February 1990, when I was in

New York to judge the Pulitzer Prizes and a call came from St. Louis saying that the reporters had gone on a byline strike. All hell was breaking loose up in the publisher's office.

The byline strike was carried out by members of the Newspaper Guild, which was then in nasty negotiations with the company over the next contract. There had been a lot of fiery rhetoric on both sides.

The journalists talked of hitting the barricades, of shutting the paper down.

The management made plans to bring in strikebreakers from our Joint Operating Agency partner, the Newhouse papers. It threatened to permanently replace any journalist who didn't cross the picket line and report for work.

The byline strike was a step short of an actual work stoppage. It was a last desperate measure before the journalists said, to hell with it, we're walking out. What happened was that the reporters, photographers, graphic artists, and anyone else in the Guild who might have a byline in the paper refused to have their names put on their work. (As a union member, Martha, of course, was part of this.) This was permissible in the existing contract. They were trying to embarrass the paper, and they succeeded.

As a result of the byline strike, the paper looked both a mess and foolish. Whereas readers had been accustomed to seeing names with stories and pictures, now all these articles and photographs and graphics were appearing as if they had materialized out of thin air. Who wrote them? What was their authority? What was going on down at the paper?

The management was furious and talked of disciplinary retaliation. The absence of bylines was affecting the credibility of the paper. It might even cost us money, managers said, if advertisers agreed with the Guild. Some executives declared the byline strikers should be fired.

What I did was write a column, supporting the byline strike. Not surprisingly, this annoyed my boss, Joseph Pulitzer, but to his credit he merely held his nose and did nothing to keep the piece out of the paper. The business-side people fumed. The editor was not supposed to be sympathetic to the union. As the British might say, I was a traitor to my class.

Until then, I had been content to think of ownership in the conventional way. The owners of our paper, or of any paper, private or publicly traded, were the shareholders, some of whom had great personal fortunes invested in the company's financial performance. Through their officers and directors, these owners made fundamental decisions affecting the paper's future. What problems need urgent attention? Where should it spend its money—on capital improvements, acquisitions, a new printing plant?

The byline strike in the *Post-Dispatch* was a protest by journalists against the take-no-prisoners negotiating tactics of the company, which they perceived as a departure from its honorable tradition. Those tactics, they said, were a repudiation of the Pulitzer Platform ("never tolerate injustice") that ran every day on the editorial page.

On one level, the strike could be described as a conventional labor action, intended to force a result at the bargaining table. But, as I told our readers, it also could be seen as something considerably more profound. On a deeper level, the strike was an assertion of ownership. It was a statement by caring journalists that they, too, were owners of the paper. And I had come to see that they were right.

Journalists are shareholders in the spirit of the newspaper and in its traditions and in the maintenance of its principles. Without these qualities, the richest paper on earth is impoverished.

The byline strike, as I saw it, was an exercise of these shareholders' rights to keep the paper on a course. It was disruptive of the day-to-day journalistic process, untidy in the questions it undoubtedly raised in the minds of the readers but ultimately as legitimate, and perhaps as necessary, as any act on the part of a paper's financial ownership to preserve the institution—in the latter case by making it profitable and competitive.

If you are wondering whether my name was on this column, it was. Firstly, the editor is not a member of the Newspaper Guild. He has many opportunities to make his views understood, at every level. More fundamentally, my column was a communication to the readers from the editor, who had to retain not only his identity but the responsibilities that went along with the job, as long as he was in it. You can't do that anonymously.

But the shareholders and the journalists are not the only owners of a newspaper. There is a third class of owners, and that is its readers. You might call these the community as shareholders. Without the support and goodwill of these owners, no paper can survive, let alone prosper. These are owners to which the management and journalists of news organizations are not always sufficiently sensitive or respectful. In countless ways the readers depend upon us. They need us for information—news of the day and commercial information.

They send forth cries for help and understanding: Pay attention to us, they implore. The claims of these shareholders are as valid as the claims of the first owners on profits or of the second ones on tradition. They arrive as complaints, as demands for better service or more consideration, as a plea to be partners in the creation of a better community.

Shareholders of wealth and property, shareholders of spirit, shareholders of community—these did not quite exhaust the list of our owners. There was, finally, the ultimate owner of the *Post-Dispatch* and every other paper in this country. That owner is America: America the idea, the democracy.

America invests in the press through the First Amendment. More than money, more than talent, more than dedication, it is this resource that allows us journalists to freely gather and print news.

It is this investment that allows us to say, without fear of official interference, what we believe to be the truth. And it is this endowment that provides us with the greatest right of all, a right that is unique to free men and women: the right to be wrong, as long as our error is not the error of malice.

If we as journalists betray the owners of wealth, we betray our material benefactors. If we betray the owners of spirit, we betray tradition. If we betray the owners of community, we betray those who depend upon us. But if we betray the ultimate owner, which is our franchise under the First Amendment, by doing less than our very best, every minute and under every circumstance, then we betray all the other shareholders and ourselves as well and all that we stand for as journalists.

Part II

The
Craft of
Journalism

8

Stacking the Deck

At our first class, I told you the story of the Baulne family of Kelowna, British Columbia, and how the aging parents, Maurice and Belva, took their lives and that of their severely disabled adult son, Reese, because of a situation that seemed terrifying and utterly hopeless. The son was thirty-four years old and had lived his life with a devastating form of epilepsy known as Lennox-Gastaut Syndrome.

The parents could place Reese in a government nursing home. Or they could go on trying to care for him, knowing that their resources were dwindling. Sooner when their money ran out or later after they were gone, the son would be put in an institution. Their effort to get five hundred dollars a month from the provincial family agency was rejected.

The excruciating dimensions of their dilemma were set down in a suicide note that authorities found in the small house trailer where the asphyxiated bodies were found. The father was unable to work because of a back injury. To leave the son to the care of strangers was unthinkable. Year by year, Maurice and Belva grew older.

Neighbors provided some information. They told of seeing the father sitting on a tractor he could no longer drive, weeping. Anyone aware of the effects of the Lennox-Gastaut form of epilepsy could imagine even more terrible details to the story. The disease makes its appearance in early childhood and is associated with mental retardation. The seizures from it can be lightning quick or persist for a long time. Patients sometimes go blank. Falls are common and always a danger for serious injury. For Lennox-Gastaut, there is no cure.

I asked Wednesday whether you thought the story of the Baulne family held material for an editorial, and you seemed to think so. When I asked what might be its theme, some of you talked about commenting on the inflexibility of government in cases where just a little help might make all the difference in the lives of suffering people. Such an approach draws upon a view of government's responsibility to its people; but it also reflects a sense of compassion. In short, you might say that such an approach arises both from the head and heart.

Now you may also remember that these elements—at least an implied assertion of government's proper role and sympathy for the Baulnes—were the ones I stressed as I told the story about the family. I was laying the groundwork for a particular kind of editorial. Some might say I was stacking the deck to produce an editorial outcome.

It was not the only way the deck could be stacked, of course. I might have told a different story, about a family that looked to government and providence to solve their problems. Reese Baulne, after all, had been diagnosed decades ago with Lennox-Gastaut. There had been many years for the Baulnes to prepare themselves financially and spiritually for this eventuality. Providence had not intervened with a cure, and the government maintains centralized health facilities for long-term care.

From this point of view, if the Baulnes were not to blame for their situation, at least they bore some responsibility for it. You can see the editorial that might have flowed from this (and perhaps have read it in the *Wall Street Journal*). Such an editorial also could be said to come from the head and heart—from an intellectual perspective on the limits of government and from a spirit hardened to anything but muscular self-reliance.

A little while ago I used the term stacking the deck, which is a bad thing to accuse card players of, for it implies cheating. Yet, I would suggest that stacking the deck is what editorial writers do routinely and usually honorably. They take the pieces of information at hand—you might think here of the cards in a deck—and arrange them in a pattern that creates a version of good or bad public policy or a particular moral perspective that they wish readers to associate with events or developments in the news.

Good editorial writers do not go beyond what they can document or verify. But within the realm of what the editorial writer believes is a reality that exists—not one they would like to exist or one that a few nips and tucks will turn into something preferable—they work with what is there and shape it in the direction their heads and hearts lead. What comes out of the deck is an editorial with a point of view.

As in all good journalism, there is a strong avoidance of conjecture or assumption. Why, really, do people kill themselves? We can never truly know, though there may be strong evidence around. If we are speculating, we need to be honest about that.

Am I saying that emotion can be a valuable part of an editorial? Absolutely. Joseph Pulitzer, my boss, believed indignation was essential for some editorials. If you can touch the hearts of your readers as well as their minds, you are much more likely to move them to action. But emotions must be tapped into wisely and kept under control. Otherwise the editorial becomes a tiresome screed or a mess of feeling from which nothing constructive can come.

It occurred to me after class Wednesday that I did not tell you whether the local papers had written editorials about the Baulnes. How could I have neglected this? One of them, the *Province* in Vancouver, provided a once-in-a-lifetime journalistic experience—unforgettable, except that I managed to forget last week. Sometimes a teacher sets out to juggle too much.

Anyway. Occasionally papers will run one-liner editorials under the headline of "Cheers and Jeers" or "Thumbs Up, Thumbs Down." *Cheers for the kids at Central High who raised enough through bake sales and car washes to send the debate team to Washington; jeers for the police officers who tried to shut down the car wash because it lacked a permit.*

I think of these as a kind of editorial graffiti, but to each editor his or her own taste. Whenever they work, it's because both sides of the equation are subjects of similar weight that can balance each other on the scales of Cheers and Jeers: good kids, thick cops. And they need to be light or humorous, requiring little thought. In any event, this is how an editorial writer in Vancouver elected to treat the deaths of the Baulnes.

About the time the Baulne story broke, there must have been something in the news about the invention of a pet washing machine. Cats and dogs would come out of this wonderful contraption alive and smelling nice and clean. What a perfect pairing for the Baulnes: Thumbs up for the new pet washing machine; thumbs down for the provincial ministry that said No when the Baulnes asked for a little money to care for their epileptic son. Is editorial writing a great business or what?

9

Writing for the Humble Heart

*Y*ears ago, there was a young reporter at the *St. Louis Post-Dispatch* named Ralph Williams. Ralph by no means was considered a star. As I recall, the only thing that set him apart was the fact that he wore a fedora, all the time. Perhaps he had the notion that this is the way big-city reporters dressed.

Unlike other young reporters who came from interesting if smaller papers or who had impressive educational credentials, Ralph had made his way into the newsroom from the advertising department. No one knew exactly how. He toiled in the zones section, wherein the mostly new reporters covered the suburbs or rewrote press releases for what was called the Sunday Inter edition. The Inter was the edition that was printed along about Friday and contained, in addition to advertising, second-echelon news items that could be set in type early in the week without fear of their being overtaken by news events. It held much of the stuffing for the real Sunday paper. For the most part, Sunday Inter copy was unrelated to news, at least as we fancier reporters thought of news.

The editor of the section, a nice old fellow named John Bell, would keep a shoebox at his desk. It was filled with press releases, and Sunday Inter reporters were expected, when they had finished with whatever assignment they were working on, to go up to Mr. Bell's desk and pick out some press releases to check out and write up for the Inter. It was modest work, and in those days almost no one got bylines. Ralph Williams was a real demon at the Sunday Inter press release work, which the other, hipper, young reporters shunned. It was beneath them. Perhaps some of them actually had master's degrees in journalism. They thought of Ralph Williams as a joke: What a laugh he was, decked out in his funny hat from Walter Winchell's era, briskly marching up to turn press releases into three-inch items for a part of the paper nobody read.

Then one day Ralph Williams said to his hipper colleagues, I see how all of you go up to Mr. Bell's shoebox and look through those press releases to find ones that you can turn into a real story. Do you know what I look for? I look for press releases from TWA or Ozark Air Lines, about some young woman who's just finished stewardess school. In those days, they did not have male flight attendants. They were all stewardesses.

Yes, he went on, I look for these pieces about stewardess school and I write them up, and do you know what? And, of course, no one did know what, since they were all busy avoiding press releases about stewardess school and the like and were looking for things that might involve "a master plan for the new urban infrastructure." I write up these items about those young women from TWA, Ralph Williams went on, and their grandmothers clip them out of the paper and carry them in their purses until the day they die.

I would like to say that Ralph Williams went on to a distinguished career, but I can't. After his stint on the zones, I lost track of him. And yet what he said to those best and brightest young reporters has stayed with me always. A lot of what we write is talked about by smart people and gets attention in high places: We may even do something to improve society. But, as Kipling said in another context, after the tumult and the shouting dies, there stands that ancient sacrifice, a humble and a contrite heart. We write for that heart and that person, too, and I don't want a single one of you to forget it. Ever.

10

Knowing Enough

Whenever I talk about my days in college, I can tell just by the look on Martha's face that she would not have cared for me back then. In truth, my friends and I must have been too precious for words. It's painful, in fact, to think back on it.

We were all English majors, and being too hip to live with the small-town Kansas boys in our fraternities, we rented a house. Naturally, we named it The Wasteland. Elizabethan poetry, jazz, sports cars, Shetland crew-necks with Eastern labels, home-brewed stout put away in Heinekens' beautiful green bottles (with the labels steamed off), going to Kansas City to hear the blues shouter Jimmy Witherspoon—those were the high-water marks of our tastes.

Those were the fifties, and we were part of what's known now as the Silent Generation. Our minds were devoid of any social or political thought. Once romantically I allowed myself to be blindfolded and initiated by candlelight into a secret organization with the forlorn mission of recapturing Republican Kansas for the Democrats. Why? Who knows? I scarcely knew the difference between the two.

Eventually, we came to the attention of the university authorities, and after repeated outrages against sobriety and community decorum we were all evicted from The Wasteland, forced to go back to "university approved housing" and placed on disciplinary probation. You'll be happy to know that's another story.

Among the things we liked to quote was W. H. Auden's Phi Beta Kappa poem of 1946 at Harvard, which he aptly subtitled "A Reactionary Tract for the Times." Toward the end of his poem, Auden had some advice that we thought was very cool:

> Thou shalt not sit
> With statisticians nor commit
> A social science.

That is how we thought of such things in those days. Statisticians were people beneath our association, and social science was something one committed, like a misdemeanor.

That also is how many journalists back in the days of the Old Order thought of statistics and social science. A good reporter, it was assumed, needed a knowledge of neither of those things. If you had an assignment coming up and you had the time, you pulled the clips from the morgue, which is how the reference library was known, and read what you could before you left the office. A good reporter was someone who, after a little small talk, could figure out a story angle with anyone he was interviewing, and later, after a couple of pops at the corner saloon, could bang out a good story. There was a strong anti-intellectual streak in the news business back then. It persists today. You still hear reporters and editors saying that journalism school is a waste of time. Whatever you need to know, you can learn it better on the job.

Partly this disdain grew out of those old bedfellows: arrogance and ignorance. Partly it was defensive. Every newsroom had its stars who never went to college but could write those who had under the table. A young woman at the *Post-Dispatch* once was overheard saying she could do multiple regression analyses and thereafter was regarded as a freak with a talent that could serve no useful purpose in a newsroom. Perhaps she belonged in a carnival, with the geek who bit the heads off chickens or the ninety-seven-pound cigarette fiend who sat shirtless in a cage and smoked ten at a time.

Partly, it was the result of the structural restraints built into journalism back then, before publishers hired attack-dog law firms to put "management rights" clauses into their contracts. (Before those clauses, Arthur Brisbane's notion of multi-tasking—a single journalist reporting and writing a story, taking photos or video for it, servicing the Web, going on TV with the story—were pipe dreams.) Contracts, for example, limited picture taking to photographers. Bad things could happen if they were ignored. I actually have seen work stoppages in the composing room because some editor had the bad judgment to actually touch a piece of type or a layout, which by contract were within the exclusive purview of compositors.

Partly, I suspect, it was a reflection of America in that day. It was not until 1965 that the percentage of white Americans who had graduated from high school crept over 50 percent. When Ray Lyle hired me at the *Kansas City Times* in 1957, fewer than 8 percent of the people had completed four or more years of college. Today, according to the Poynter Institute for Media Studies, 90 percent of journalists are college graduates.

Today, it's also unremarkable to find reporters with masters degrees competing for entry-level jobs. Newsrooms are not only more educated than they've ever been, they're smarter, too.

These thoughts began taking place last Friday as we listened to Griff Palmer of the *San Jose Mercury News* talk about databases and how journalists today who know nothing of using spreadsheets quickly get lost in dealing with basic public information that increasingly comes in computer formats. Auden's witty remarks in the year after World War II may have been harmless in that time, but today any journalist taking them seriously would be committing professional suicide.

Even so, our professional journalism curriculums badly lag behind the times. You can easily get a graduate degree in journalism from good universities without having to take courses in statistics or social science research methodologies. This needs to change, not just in the professional education of journalists but in our newsrooms.

T. S. Eliot once said of another poet that he had a fine ear for language, but what a pity it was that he didn't know enough. (Was it Wordsworth? Longfellow?) How true it is of us. By and large, we journalists write well enough. By and large, we learn with experience how to make it through a complicated interview or subject and write about it in a way that the ordinary person can understand and perhaps even enjoy. But the pity is, we don't know enough.

Most newsrooms today have their medical writer. But how often do we see him or her in the spare moments going through the *New England Journal of Medicine*? Is the science writer up on the current issue of *Nature*? Is the *American Journal of Sociology* on the news organization's subscription list? Is the farm writer conversant with the *American Journal of Agricultural Economics*? You get the idea. My dream in St. Louis was that our specialists would know as much or more about their areas as anyone outside academia.

Of course that never happened. It required an investment in money and time and energy that few newspapers can or are willing to commit. There are professional seminars and workshops to attend. There are mini-courses at universities to enroll in. There are more meetings, speakers, symposiums, and so forth than any journalist can keep up with. There are books to buy, databases to acquire, journals to subscribe to. And, of course, there is the insatiable appetite of the profession, which manifests itself in the next day's paper, 365 times a year. The conscientious journalist endures the torture of King Sisyphus, forever doomed never to finish the task.

You hear a great deal of talk nowadays about changes in journalism. Mostly they involve the effects of technology or the consolidation of media ownership or the inexorable pressures on news that are coming from the stock market–driven demands for short-term profits. You do not hear much about the intellectual or knowledge-based changes that are necessary if we are to be able to "tell what happened," as Ray Lyle demanded. If we are to be able to understand reality sufficiently to create Walter Lippmann's picture of it upon which people can act. If we are to know enough.

Like all change for the better, this one does not require a Cultural Revolution in which every artifact and practice of the past must be repudiated. I hope to show you that there is much in our tradition that remains valuable and, yes, even essential. The trick in effective change is learning what from the past should be retained and what should be replaced. I do not want a newsroom in which the learned specialist reporter has driven out the journalist with a magic touch at the keyboard. We need both. But until the golden wordsmith and the scholar journalist are working side by side, our newsrooms will not be adequate.

11

The People Watching in the Distance

Many years ago, I was in Saigon to do a story on what it was like for American civilians as the city grew increasingly unstable and dangerous. This was in the spring of 1964, more than a year before the first big U.S. troop increase was announced. By now there were bombings and grenade attacks, and in their compounds and neighborhoods American families were training themselves to be self-defense forces.

I was going to be a very short-timer there, and as I sat at sidewalk bars, I would wonder naively if the next bicycle rider might drop something nasty off at my table. But all anyone ever tried to lay on me were dirty pictures.

I went to lunch at the home of a man who was a mid-level, non-policy officer at the U.S. Embassy. They were midwesterners—he, his wife, and their three children—and at home the kids would have been at public school, and I imagined a night out for the parents would have been dinner or cards with friends.

In Saigon, they lived in a nine-room house in a lane off Rue Pasteur. There was a lovely walled garden in which the bougainvillea, hibiscus, and frangipani were blooming. They kept a black gibbon named Jocko in a cage, and they had many exotic birds. They also had four servants.

Before lunch, the servants came in with frosted, stemmed glasses containing excellent frozen daiquiris. After bringing us our drinks, the servants withdrew. But throughout my visit I sensed their presence and watchfulness, these Vietnamese who came and went quietly, doing their work efficiently and expressionlessly; and I knew that we had no business there in what was their place.

I had seen the look nearly twenty years before. When World War II ended and the American military ended the Japanese occupation in Shanghai, my mother got a job as a secretary with Shanghai Port Command, whose job was to keep troops and supplies moving. One Saturday, some officers took us on a picnic in Longhua, a nearby place known for its old pagoda and wonderful flat peaches. My grandfather once had a summer house there, but it was lost in the war.

We went out in jeeps and there was good food in hampers, and china, linen, and silverware, too. What I remember most vividly, though, was the large crowd of poorly dressed Chinese that suddenly materialized and watched closely every move we made. They were utterly silent.

The officers had the drivers shoo them away, but they returned, standing a little ways off, staring at us with expressions that were part curiosity and part reproach. I remember feeling acutely uncomfortable, as if we the picnickers were intruders, with no business being there in what was their place.

Why am I telling you these things? What do they have to do with our immediate common endeavor, which is the writing of commentary? You have been writing editorials mostly about public policies and now you will be writing essays and columns, and though there will be plenty involving policy, you will also be looking at humanity and within yourselves. It is for the latter reason that I've begun this letter in this way.

Ever since I was a child, I have been sensitive to the people in the distance, watching, understanding more than I do about their place in the world and mine. I am grateful I did not lose the trait, because it helped me as a journalist. It helps me realize the isolated nature of our calling and how we must both respect the distance from which we observe and how hard we must work to bridge that gap, to understand, and to communicate that understood reality to our readers.

You probably know that great passage from the set of devotions John Donne wrote shortly before he died in 1623: *No man is an island, entire of itself; every man is a piece of the continent, a part of the main; if a clod be washed away by the sea, Europe is the less* . . . And then comes the words that still retain the power to send a chill through us: . . . *any man's death diminishes me, because I am involved in mankind, and therefore never send to know for whom the bell tolls; it tolls for thee.*

Every journalist should commit this to heart, for it not only says that we are a part of the vast whole of humankind, but that the loss of any of that whole affects us as well as everyone else. Even more: What happens to that whole matters, whether it is joyous, tragic, or as day-after-day in the routine as are sunshine, rain, and the changing seasons and heavens.

So now young writers of op-ed essays and columns, remember this. Humanity is inseparable from everything else. Every piece of public policy has its human component. The more we are able to connect that human component with the policy—be it taxes, defense, crime and punishment, whatever—the more it will mean to our readers, both to an understanding of their own place in America but also that of their neighbors and the millions of men and women they will never meet.

How do we connect those things? By becoming wiser about life, of course, though that usually requires experience. By understanding the details and implications of policies, too; for if the numbers confuse us, if the details bore us, we can never write with any authority about them. Our attempts to connect them with people will never amount to more than pointless anecdotal ledes or lame efforts to universalize issues from wildly insufficient samples. By reading the news daily, by talking about the news, by becoming interested in documents and specialized writing that will give us the background we need.

All of this, of course, is terribly difficult. The good news is that we need not attempt the impossible, if we write naturally and simply. If the words we use are sturdy and work for a living and are not loafing around, our sentences taking up space and consuming energy. If we have a clear idea of what needs to be said and then do our best to set it down without pretense or grandiose design, we can usually succeed. With each modest success, our confidence increases, as does our competence.

Among our best tools as writers about humanity are our own senses. Observe. Listen. Sniff the air. Taste the food you are writing about. Stand or sit still and quietly, and see how much of the world you can take in. Remember the people watching silently from the distance and try to understand what you may mean to them. Write these things down.

Draw little pictures, crude if necessary, of the house that burned or the wooded hills at the edge of the field into which the children wandered on a sunny afternoon that has turned into their parents' heartbreak. You can never re-create these things from imagination. Only reporting provides such tools.

Do not be afraid of your feelings and thoughts but remember they are always in the service of your article. Commentary writing, as I told you earlier, is not a self-directed activity; it is not the hermit's natural expression. You are offering to others a view of the world, which is an opinion. It is not an exhibition of your soul's interior decoration.

12

Simple Writing Is Not Easy Writing

Well before he became known as a playwright, George Bernard Shaw was a journalist, a music critic for London papers. He wrote under the pseudonym of Corno di Basetto, which is the Italian for the tenor clarinet or basset horn. It is said that Shaw thought the name sounded like a fancy European title.

Shaw loved Mozart, as I do, and was indignant that so little of his music was played. People dismissed his music as too simple, as "tuneful little trifles," he wrote.

Shaw knew the real reason there was not much Mozart in the music halls. Far from being simple, his music was terribly difficult to do well. In 1891, the one hundredth anniversary of Mozart's death, Shaw wrote that only the finest execution would serve "whilst, at the same time, your work is so obvious, that everyone thinks it must be easy, and puts you down remorselessly as a duffer for botching it."

It is the same with writing. Much of great writing is simple writing, and as with Mozart's music, it is devilishly hard to do. No one understood this better than T. S. Eliot, whose lines on writing from East Coker I carry in my wallet:

> And so each new venture
> Is a new beginning, a raid on the inarticulate
> With shabby equipment always deteriorating
> In the general mess of imprecision of feeling . . .

In my comments on your first article, there was a persistent theme. Simplify, simplify, simplify. Let the facts, let the details, tell the story. That's all we really have to do. Set them down simply. William Zinsser writes how the English language is strangling in "unnecessary words, circular constructions, pompous frills and meaningless jargon." Read any newspaper and you can see what he means.

Simple writing is not easy writing, though the elements of simple writing are what we've used since childhood. All we're about as writers are nouns, some verbs, a few adjectives, and a little punctuation, assembled in the most efficient manner. To be effective writers, we must know the meaning of every word we use. We don't need dictionaries for fancy words as much as we need them for the ordinary ones.

A few years ago, I gave a talk at the National Writers Workshop, which is put on by the Poynter Institute and newspapers here and there. This one was in Wilmington, Delaware. I began with a parable that I'd invented. It went like this.

Once upon a time there lived a king who loved to eat. He kept the finest table in the world, presided over by the finest chef who ever lived. Life was good, but dinner was even better. Then one day the master of the royal kitchen came to the king and said, "I am growing old and must return to my village."

The king was sad, and he asked one favor of the old man. "Stay one more week," he said, "and cook for me dishes that I'll remember forever."

The chef thanked the king and set to work. He made roasts and ragouts, cassoulets and cakes, soups and sauces, puddings and profiteroles. Each one was wonderful. But after every meal, the king would say, "Can you cook something that is better still?"

So it came to pass that the week ended. There was only one more meal to be served. The old man returned to the kitchen, and there he took from the royal pantry . . . a potato. And he took, too, a little bit of salt and a little bit of pepper and, almost as an afterthought, a little bit of the butter that was always there on the royal countertop in the royal kitchen. And then he set about to make a boiled potato fit for the king.

After all the seasonings and all the sauces, after all of the preparations and all of the presentations, it came down to the simplest thing: a boiled potato that had to be done exactly right. Now a boiled potato cannot be disguised or made to seem that it is something grander than it is. It is there, itself, plain, devoid of ornamentation and pretense.

The boiled potato, the old man said, was the culmination of all he had learned. And the king, though he was hard to satisfy, as kings often are, ate the boiled potato and said he had never tasted anything better.

In my own way, I am still trying to make that boiled potato. I have spent nearly fifty years in journalism and I am still trying to write a simple declarative sentence—one which, if I had a king and I wished to go to my rest, I could put before him as the summation of all the things I have learned: a sentence that was just right, a thing of itself, full and complete, devoid of all pretense, a subject and a verb and the merest sprinkling of salt and of pepper—a sentence that would be a joy to read with every fact in it chaste and immaculate.

Now a good declarative sentence, of course, is made up of words. And just like the boiled potato of our story, all the ingredients that go into it have to be just right. If you love words, as I do, you think of them as your inheritance, never to be squandered, never to be wasted.

But although words are a writer's most precious possessions, it's how we use them that makes all the difference. As I said, we're only talking about nouns and verbs and adjectives and adverbs, held together with commas and semicolons and periods—what you might call the double helix, or the basic building blocks, of all writing.

If we use words imprecisely, without attention to their meaning, then the sentences in which they appear will be imprecise. They will not mean what we imagine they mean or want them to mean. And the sentences will look like woodworking with the joints poorly assembled, with pieces crudely jammed together. There will be no craftsmanship to our writing, no fit-and-finish.

Yet, unlike the craftsman who makes furniture with fine tools and out of good wood, the conditions of our labor, as Eliot reminds us, involve shabby equipment that always deteriorates, words that crack and break under the tension, a constant, unwinnable battle against the inarticulate. What we are about, you students and I, is terribly difficult.

When I began this letter, I hadn't intended for it to have focused so much on Eliot, but he's on my mind now, and I'll offer a few more lines. These bear on the heart of our enterprise and they are from "Little Gidding," another of the Quartets:

> Ash on an old man's sleeve
> Is all the ash the burnt roses leave.
> Dust in the air suspended
> Marks the place where a story ended.

You can look on those lines as a kind of reporter's credo—to note detail and find a way to write about it: the ash on an old man's sleeve, the dust suspended and a story that ended. That is what Ray Lyle meant by telling me to just write what happened, down to the smallest detail. Who is the old man? How did the roses burn? Why is dust in the air? Tell me the story and how it ended. And do it as simply as you can, as simply as that lovely passage from Eliot, where of the twenty-six words I quoted, only three have more than one syllable.

I hope as you write as journalists you'll remember some of these things we'll be about in this class—to report carefully, to think before you type, to use the words we use every day and not those we save for company.

A simple declarative thing is a humble thing, though magnificent in the hands of great writers—just as a boiled potato is a humble dish, though sometimes fit for a king. It all depends on the care we give them, the honesty with which we approach our task, the respect we have for the simple tools of our trade, which are the words and which, if we are wise, we look upon as treasures.

13
Choosing the Right Words

I was happily reading one of your articles Sunday morning. It was good enough to persuade me to vote for someone I hadn't planned on supporting. It brought the candidate to life and gave me the facts I needed. So far, terrific. A nice grade lay in its future. And then there came a line that contained something about an after-school program for *at-risk students.* And suddenly my blood ran cold.

When I recovered, I finished the piece and the grade was still a good one. But it took me awhile to get happy again. I've spoken a bit about what I think of jargon, sociobabble, euphemisms, and other fashionable blemishes on good writing. I think of them as the Botox of writing. It may seem to help for a little while but then things start sagging again.

This is as good a time as any to talk about Botox writing, and I'd begin by directing you to a useful Web site run by the Edna McConnell Clark Foundation. It's called The Jargon Finder.

Let's turn to *at-risk:*

This mystifying expression owes its popularity to one embarrassing fact: The phrase almost always designates a category of people of whom it is awkward to speak honestly. Almost every branch of charity or human service uses AT-RISK to describe the people whom its practitioners are . . . well, worried about. Here is one sample definition, from Education Week:

"AT-RISK describes a student with socioeconomic challenges, such as poverty or teen pregnancy, which may place them [sic] at a disadvantage in achieving academic, social, or career goals. Such students are deemed 'at risk' of failing, dropping out, or 'falling through the cracks.'"

Generalize from education to other fields of social concern, and AT-RISK becomes simply the polite euphemism for "headed into trouble." But in today's etiquette of upbeat and respectful neutrality, it would be considered grotesquely prejudicial, not to say hostile, to describe people that way. AT-RISK, however, is regarded as abstract enough to be polite, even in mixed company.

When I first taught this course, I would take the students to Sacramento for a day. We'd begin with a session with the political editors of the *Sacramento Bee* and then we'd head over to the Capitol, where Byron Sher, then a Democratic state senator from Palo Alto, would talk to us. After lunch in the Capitol restaurant, the students would do reporting on stories that had angles in Sacramento, and late in the afternoon we'd tootle back to Stanford.

One year, the students asked if I'd arrange a tour of the Capitol. Of course. So I called the tour information line of the California State Capitol Museum.

The line was answered automatically and I was given a list of options. There was a number to call for "the deaf community."

Now just exactly what was the message trying to say? That to get in touch with the "deaf community," you should call this number? That deaf tourists should call this number? I think that was the more likely of the two, but those responsible for the message couldn't bring themselves to say it plainly. Deaf community sounds so much nicer. It's a euphemism.

What's a euphemism? A word or a phrase that is less expressive or direct but is considered more tasteful or less offensive. Now, is our aim to be offensive and tasteless? No. It is to be clear. It is to use the right words. If people we interview say things like *at-risk* and we're not using a direct quote, for heaven's sakes recast the sentence. Don't let them put Botox into our writing.

One of the best examples of euphemisms in journalism is the ubiquitous *community*. As in the deaf community, or the homeless community, the African American community, the Asian community, the gay-lesbian-bisexual-transgender community, the medical community, the religious community . . . You read it in the papers everyday. I probably use it myself, when I'm not thinking carefully about what I'm saying.

We see stories about appeals made to the "international community" instead of to the world. We see stories about various issues affecting the African American community. Now there are certain issues that may affect all black Americans or African Americans, in which case, why not just say that? Otherwise it suggests a homogeneity of interests or economic or social class that simply doesn't exist.

What's objectionable about that? It's imprecise, for one thing, and when writing is unclear it is a dead giveaway for unclear thinking. What else? It suggests that everyone is alike. We're all one big happy community, made up of smaller and smaller communities. It implies something positive. It sounds nice. It grants people an identity—makes them, if you will, part of a community.

Sometimes it's exactly the right word and then you should use it. Webster's says that community is 1. All the people in a particular district, city. 2. A group of people living together as a smaller social unit within a larger one, and having interests, work, etc. in common . . .

A few years ago, after the U.S. Department of Education issued one of its periodic directives, there was an interesting reaction from the National Federation of the Blind, representing, as some journalists would say, the blind community. The memo began by recalling that the 1992 Rehabilitation Act Amendments had officially replaced the term "handicap" with the term "disability."

The memo went on to say that the U.S. Office of Civil Rights recognizes "the preference of individuals with disabilities to use phraseology that stresses the individuality of all children, youth, and adults, and then the incidence of a disability. In all our written and oral communications, care should be given to avoid expressions that many persons find offensive." (This was a sentence written by an English-speaking adult who may well have had more than one college degree.)

So instead of disabled persons, all communications should refer to "Persons with a disability" or "individuals with disabilities." Instead of deaf persons, writers should make it "Persons who are deaf" or "people with hearing impairments." And instead of blind people, it should be "People who are blind" or "persons with a visual impairment." Ray Lyle would notice immediately that, in addition to what linguists call "bleaching," in every case two words have been replaced by four or five.

Now you might think that this would have been greeted with appreciation by the blind community. In fact, just the opposite occurred.

The National Federation of the Blind adopted a resolution that began with these words, "Whereas the word blind accurately and clearly describes the condition of being unable to see . . ." The resolution stated that there was increasing pressure to use a variety of euphemisms in referring to blindness or blind people—euphemisms such as "hard of seeing, visually challenged, sightless, visually impaired, people who are blind and the like . . ."

Moreover, the resolution observed that differentiations must be made among these euphemisms (visually impaired or visually limited imply a slight ability to see; they don't mean blind, as Webster means blind, as without the power of sight, unable to see) and declared that such circumlocutions are deserving only of ridicule to avoid straightforward, respectable words such as blind, blindness, the blind.

The resolution acknowledged the intention of these euphemisms to make people feel better by noting that the word "person" must invariably precede the word blind to emphasize the fact that a blind person is first and foremost a person. In fact, the federation declared that exactly the opposite effect occurs, for it suggests that blind people are overly defensive, shameful of their condition, and are touchy and belligerent. Bankers, the resolution said, are not ashamed of being called bankers instead of persons in the banking business.

So the resolution concluded:

> We believe it is respectable to be blind, and although we have no particular pride in the fact of our blindness, neither do we have any shame in it. To the extent that euphemisms are used to convey any other concept or image, we deplore such use. We can make our own way in the world on equal terms.

The late Kenneth Jernigan, the president of the federation, had a few words of his own to add to this, and I implore you to take them to heart. Here's what he said:

> Euphemisms and the politically correct language which they exemplify are sometimes only prissy, sometimes ridiculous, and sometimes tiresome. Often, however, they are more than that. At their worst they obscure clear thinking and damage the very people and causes they claim to benefit.

14

The Use of Advance Copy: An Example

Some of you have yet to cast your first vote for a president of the United States. Though all of you are young, others may already be veteran voters. I remember my first vote vividly. It was for John F. Kennedy.

This November, when we elect the president, America will also observe the forty-first anniversary of Kennedy's murder. When the twenty-fifth anniversary came around in 1988, I was the editor of the *St. Louis Post-Dispatch*, and I went to Dallas to write something about it. I say *something* because what came out was a very different kind of article: part reportage, part reminiscence, part political analysis. That was one of the benefits of being the editor; you could write pieces like this.

I'm sending it to you as your letter this week because it has an appropriate fit for the election season. That this one has produced strong and sometimes ugly passions is nothing new. Kennedy was hated by many people in a way so vehement as to make the feelings about the incumbent seem mild by comparison.

I'm sending it to you also because you've been introduced to A-copy, parts of a story prepared in advance of an expected event, and I want you to see how much A-copy there is in this story—how much homework the writer did before even leaving for Dallas. The A-copy begins right after the sentence about Parkland Hospital, where Kennedy died, that says: *Hospital records show that on the day Kennedy died, 18 babies were born.*

The A-copy is suspended as the reporter describes the gathering twilight in Dealey Plaza and then picks up again briefly with the lovely quote from Bobby Kennedy before ending right before the last graph. There the writer returns to the flock of black birds, which have a symbolic place in this story. Note the verb *keening,* to describe the noise of the birds. A keen, the noun, is a lamentation for the dead; keening, the verb, is a loud mournful sound made by the bereaved.

And note, too, the importance the reporter placed on detail throughout the story.

By William F. Woo

© 1988 *St. Louis Post-Dispatch,* reprinted with permission

DALLAS—This, then, is the place, where the street names and buildings are engraved in memory, where John F. Kennedy, the president, came riding through a cheering crowd and where, at 12:30 p.m., a quarter century ago today, he was shot and fatally wounded.

This, then, is the place where the nightmare began.

It is Sunday, two days before the anniversary, and the weather is remarkably as it was that day in 1963: a gray, gloomy beginning, giving way to sunshine that warms the chilly air. There are no crowds here in Dealey Plaza. Nearly 40,000 people have gone to Texas Stadium to see the Dallas Cowboys play football, but here, on the last weekend before the 25th anniversary of the assassination, there are no more than 50 people at any time.

They point to the southeast corner window on the sixth floor of the Romanesque old Texas School Book Depository building, where Lee Harvey Oswald waited with his mail-order rifle. They point to the place on Elm Street, where Kennedy was struck.

The triple underpass just ahead, and the Trinity River valley beyond, were the last things the president could have seen. Children are playing on the famous grassy knoll. This high ground above the Trinity is where the city was laid out and the first house and store in Dallas were put up. And if Oswald had co-conspirators, it is from here that they fired on the president. Two hundred yards east of this place stands the Kennedy Memorial, a concrete cenotaph, symbolizing an empty tomb.

All that it contains is a block of black granite, bearing the name John Fitzgerald Kennedy, cut in gold. Above the name lies a single pink rose. Perhaps a dozen people are here. Among them are two young men, drinking beer.

A little later in the afternoon, there will be a memorial service by men who served in the Special Forces, and, incongruously, the beer drinkers will materialize to hold four sprays of flowers.

On the day Kennedy was shot, a full page advertisement in the *Dallas Morning News* asked, "Why have you ordered or permitted your brother Bobby, the Attorney General, to go soft on Communists . . . ?" Now, ironically, that accusation finds a ghostly echo at the Kennedy Memorial. At the service, an old Green Beret pledges that he and his comrades will forever fight communism, wherever it may be found. Then the president of the anticommunist American Freedom Foundation stands and quotes from the slain president's Inaugural Address: ". . . We shall pay any price, bear any burden, meet any hardship . . . to assure the survival and success of liberty."

A few miles away, at Parkland Memorial Hospital, where Kennedy was pronounced dead, the emergency room receiving docks are much as they were that day. When Kennedy arrived, he was given patient number 24740, and his condition was still undetermined.

It is 127 steps from the emergency room doors to Trauma Room One, now an X-ray chamber, where he was taken: a left turn down a tan, concrete block hall, a right, another left, about 43 seconds in all. After that, they knew there was no more hope. Hospital records show that on the day Kennedy died, 18 babies were born. The news of Kennedy's shooting traveled with unprecedented speed. In the half hour between the time that he was hit by the bullets and pronounced dead, 68 percent of adult Americans had heard of the shooting.

In less than two hours, 92 percent of the public was aware of the events in Dallas. By 6 p.m., the figure had reached 99.8 percent. The shock was immediate, profound and lasting. To a degree unmatched in the deaths of other presidents, Kennedy's loss was felt personally.

Social scientists have determined that the most common immediate association that people expressed with the dead president was a familial one. He was a father, a son, a husband, a brother—and highly visible in each role. But this was far more than a family tragedy, for Kennedy had made himself a youthful symbol of optimism, renewal, national vigor, self-sacrifice, and idealism.

He had done this consciously, introducing the concept of a New Frontier in his speech accepting the presidential nomination. The New Frontier, he said, "sums up not what I intend to offer the American people, but what I intend to ask of them."

Kennedy returned to that theme at his inauguration, and today Americans not yet born that November day can recite his most famous words: "And so, my fellow Americans: Ask not what your country can do for you—ask what you can do for your country." Over and over again, in that dark moment and ever since, Americans have lamented a loss of national innocence, of purpose and of the hope of fulfillment.

Sen. Daniel Patrick Moynihan, D-N.Y., then the assistant secretary of labor, said, "I don't think there's any point in being Irish if you don't know the world is going to break your heart eventually. I guess that we thought we had a little more time. . . . Mary McGrory said to me that we'll never laugh again. And I said, 'Heavens, Mary. We'll laugh again. It's just that we'll never be young again.'"

A few days ago, two St. Louisans in their fifties were talking, over lunch, about the assassination. Like so many others who recall the day, they could remember exactly where they were and what they were doing at the moment they heard the news.

One of them, who had not known Moynihan's remarks, summed up his own feelings in these words: "I went home and told my wife that we would never be young again."

Kennedy had won election by the barest of margins, only 113,057 votes out of 68,832,778 cast. Yet after the first month of his presidency, 72 percent of the respondents in a Gallup Poll approved of him. To an astonishing degree, that affection has remained.

To appreciate the power of the Kennedy legend, one need only look at the polls today showing that Americans believe he was the country's greatest president, greater than Washington, Jefferson, Lincoln, and all the rest. When he died, John F. Kennedy was just 46 years old and had been in office a little more than 1,000 days.

Since 1958, political scientists at the University of Michigan have been measuring the American people's trust and confidence in government. That year, only 23 percent of the public believed that they could not trust government to do the right thing most of the time. While Kennedy was president, that figure declined even further. But beginning in 1964, the year after he died, the Michigan political scientists found that confidence in government had begun to wane.

When Richard M. Nixon was elected president in 1968, the distrust index stood at 36 percent. By Watergate, it had reached 62 percent. In 1980, it had risen to 73 percent. With the election of Ronald Reagan in 1980, confidence appeared to pick up. The distrust index began to fall. But in the mid-1980s, it rose again, and by 1986, the public held essentially the same level of confidence in government that it had when Nixon resigned in 1974.

So a statistical case can be made that hope, faith, and confidence in government have never been the same since Kennedy was murdered. However apt the comparison between the Kennedy years and Camelot may have been, few could disagree that such an association would be inappropriate with the succeeding presidencies: that of Lyndon B. Johnson, wrecked by Vietnam; of Nixon, ruined by Watergate; of Jimmy

Carter and Gerald R. Ford, both repudiated by the voters; of Reagan, bedeviled by the deficit and Iran-Contra.

The succession of failed or buffeted presidencies can help explain the decline in national confidence, as also can a sequence of convulsive events that shook America, beginning with the death of Kennedy. The subsequent murders of his brother, Robert, and the Rev. Martin Luther King Jr. seemed to provide a frightening validation of assassination as a political solution.

There was violence and unrest in the cities and the campuses. Vietnam divided the nation as it had not been divided since the Civil War. The corruption of the presidency in Watergate was the utter antithesis of Camelot.

And even as these things occurred, other corrosive events were taking place: the loss of energy independence, the loss of domestic markets to Asian competitors, an explosive deficit that made America a debtor nation and a tragedy in space, the last physical realm in which the nation took its superiority for granted.

No one can say if Kennedy would have made a difference. He died even as these tumultuous forces were gathering. But while he lived, Americans believed in their government as they never have since.

Now the twilight descends upon Dallas and Dealey Plaza. The sun has set and the orange brick surface of the old Texas School Book Depository building no longer seems to glow, as it did in the bright afternoon. Only a few sightseers remain.

A hot dog vendor in front of the old Depository building packs his wares. A Texan is explaining to a Japanese family just where and how the president was shot. Suddenly the sky is alive with birds, huge flocks of black birds.

They are grackles, and there are thousands of them, everywhere one looks. The branches of the live oaks bordering the grassy knoll are full of birds. As flocks wheel across the sky, they blot out the last rays of the sun. The noise is piercing and continuous.

The Kennedy Memorial is empty of visitors now. The floral sprays from the Green Beret ceremony have been placed on the granite slab, as has been a pot of yellow and purple chrysanthemums. The pink rose, now wilting, lies in the center of the granite.

Soon the stars begin to appear. They are visible from the interior of the roofless cenotaph. President Kennedy, it has been written, talked often about the stars. They had a special meaning for him, for as a young

PT boat skipper, he had depended on them to navigate his way home in the Solomon Islands.

In the year after he was murdered, his brother Robert had alluded to the stars in a tribute delivered at the 1964 Democratic Convention. Robert Kennedy had found his inspiration in the third act of "Romeo and Juliet:"

> . . . When he shall die, take him and cut him out in little stars, And he will make the face of heaven so fine that all the world will be in love with night . . .

In the growing darkness, huge numbers of birds are still overhead. The noise is frightening. Only a few cars drive by, but the sound of traffic cannot be heard over the keening of the birds.

15

Stay with Your Story

*I*n just about every class so far, I've spoken a lot about fundamentals, and how a man named Ray Lyle at the *Kansas City Times* taught them to me many years ago. You may be tired of hearing me talk about them. Yet, I do not know of any way to get good at journalism other than respecting them.

It's the same in other endeavors. The great cellist Pablo Casals, it was said, practiced the scales every day of his life until he died. The humble things we do over and over again become like bonds of steel that keep our work from sundering. Dramatic accomplishments bring the crowd to its feet, but simple homely competence is what carries the day. A baseball team that relies on the home run may or may not win the World Series. The team that cannot field the routine ground ball will never get there.

Here are two stories about fundamentals and journalism. I have shared them with other students, but the lessons in them remain fresh and strong for me. One of them is about a success, the other about a failure, at least how failure is often thought of. The first is a story about a piece that got into the paper. The second is about one that didn't but became more important to me than almost anything I ever wrote. You may have an experience like that yourself some day.

I. Follow the Long Shot

In 1961, Lyndon Johnson, then John F. Kennedy's vice president, came to Kansas City to give a speech on education. This was a big story, and I longed to be among the reporters assigned to it.

I wasn't. The reporters who went off to the Muehlebach, the big hotel where Johnson was staying and speaking, were all veterans. I was writing items for the back of the paper.

Then from the police scanner came the electrifying news. The Muehlebach was on fire! Ray Lyle scrambled what remained of his staff, and I raced downtown. When I got to the hotel, there were police and firefighters everywhere. I looked around, picked my moment, and nonchalantly walked inside. If I got arrested, so be it. The vice president might still be there.

As inconspicuously as I could, I made my way through the lobby. I saw two men in dark suits—Secret Service agents—carrying the big vice presidential seal, the one that goes on the lectern when he speaks. They slipped out the side door, and I said to myself, "If you follow the vice president's seal, you will come to the vice president." It was a long shot, but it was the only one I had.

From a distance, I followed the agents east on Twelfth, past Main, past Walnut. Then my heart sank. A black sedan, escorted by police cars with flashing lights, pulled to the curb. The Secret Service men got in, and I watched them drive away. I'd had a good idea and I'd tried, and that was that.

But then another dark car pulled over and a familiar voice said, "Brother Woo?" It was the mayor, H. Roe Bartle, who knew me because I was the substitute City Hall reporter. Bartle was a colorful man, a Southern Baptist deacon, if I remember right, a terrific orator, and he loved the press. "Brother Woo," he said. "Do you want to go to the airport?" Did I? I jumped in the car, and we were on our way to Municipal Airport.

There, parked off to the side of the terminal, was the big blue-and-white Boeing 707 with the words "The United States of America" on the side. I followed the mayor up and into the most luxurious cabin I had ever seen. And there, coming down the aisle, was a tall man in a beautifully cut gray suit. "Mr. Vice President," the mayor said. "This is Bill Woo of the *Kansas City Star.*"

We shook hands and I froze. I couldn't think of a thing to say. Then I heard myself speak and nearly died of mortification. What I was saying was, "Sir, have you ever been run out of a hotel by a fire before?" Lyndon Johnson looked at me kindly. "Son," he said. "I've never been run out of any damned place in my life, and you can quote me."

We had a useful little conversation after that, and then it was over. I made myself wait until the jet had taken off before I called the office. Mr. Lyle got on the line and growled into the phone: "Where've you been?"

And coolly, as if I'd rehearsed the line all my life, I replied, "I've been interviewing the vice president." I was the only reporter at the paper to have talked to Lyndon Johnson.

Moral: Stay with your story, even if it looks hopeless. Maybe you'll catch a break. You won't, for sure, if you quit on it.

II. The Day JFK Was Buried

On a Friday in November 1963, I left the *Post-Dispatch* early and stopped off at the bank. I was on vacation and going to Washington to see a girlfriend. As the teller was getting my money, there was a commotion in the back, and she came running out, saying, "The president's been shot."

I drove across Illinois and Indiana in a steady rain. There were lots of stretches where in those days there were no interstate highways, and in the small towns, you saw soggy American flags tied to the parking meters. I had a little radio along, propped on the dash, and through the static I got the news from Dallas. It was an awful gray day that turned into an awful black night. John F. Kennedy was the first president I had ever voted for, and like millions of other Americans I felt sick, through and through.

When I got to Pittsburgh, I called our bureau in Washington and introduced myself. I said I was going to Washington and would do anything I could to help. That was the way I had learned it in Kansas City. If there's a big story, you pitch in. They were surprised to hear from me, but they thanked me and said, show up early Monday morning.

So I would be covering the funeral of John F. Kennedy. I was going to write my story onto page one, and people in St. Louis would know what it was like in Washington, that historic day. I would give them detail, a sense of the tragic moment. It would happen because I would do the reporting the way Mr. Lyle had taught.

When I got to the office Monday, they had an assignment for me. There were a million errands to run, and they were glad I was there for them. No, of course there wasn't a story for me. What they needed was a gopher. I was crushed, but if you're the junior hand on deck, it's bad form to complain about your assignment.

The *Post-Dispatch* had hired the historian Barbara Tuchman to write about the funeral procession and burial at Arlington National Cemetery. In the opening of her book *The Guns of August* she had written a moving account of the funeral of Edward VII. The paper wanted her to do something similar for JFK. She needed a pass to get on the press bus to Arlington, and my first errand was to go to the White House and fetch it.

And thus it happened that I found myself walking up the great circular driveway of the White House that cold, clear morning. There was nobody near. I stopped to take the scene in, and suddenly the doors of the White House opened and out into the sunlight walked the widow, Jacqueline Kennedy, all in black, and Robert Kennedy, who was holding her arm, and the children, John F. Kennedy, Jr., and Caroline. I saw them come out, to bury a husband, a father, a brother, a president of the United States.

Barbara Tuchman was at the Mayflower Hotel, where the bureau chief, Marquis Childs, had taken a suite overlooking the procession route on Connecticut Avenue. I got off the elevator, and there in front of me, in a bulky gray overcoat and looking as if he needed a shave, was Richard Nixon, the man Kennedy had defeated. We stared at each other, as people do when an elevator door opens, and then he moved past me and got on.

When I got to the suite, Mrs. Childs opened the door. "Mark," she said, "the *boy* from the *Post-Dispatch* is here," and again I felt the air go out of me. "No, dear," said Mark, ensuring heaven. "He's Bill Woo, one of our good young feature writers."

He invited me in and we chatted for a few minutes and then I went out again, to prowl the funeral route, taking notes, writing down details, watching the foreign dignitaries like Charles de Gaulle and interviewing ordinary people, all on the chance that some of it might be used by the reporters writing the story. It wasn't. Not a word of mine got in the paper, but I shall never forget that day, as long as I live.

Moral: If you're a reporter, go for the story. Volunteer. Be there. Even the humblest assignment can go into your memory forever.

16

We Dissect a Column

Even though we're moving from commentaries to columns, I'm going to revisit an unsuccessful Valentine's Day op-ed article we read in class. In this letter, I am going to try to dissect it a little more. From beginning to end, there are lessons for us.

"Would that love were simple," was the headline over this 730-word piece. At the center of the commentary lay a conversation between a man and a woman who complained chronically about her former husband. When asked why she married him, she replied, "He was the first man ever to tell me he loved me." The man was stunned. In twelve words, he said, she had given him the history of love.

You awarded the piece the lowest score ever recorded to that moment in our class. What I hope is that beyond the visceral response to the piece, there was also learning in it for you. That's why I'm bringing it up again here.

As I've mentioned to you, on op-ed pages, the boundaries between commentaries by outside writers and columns by staff or professional journalists are increasingly indistinct. As I also said, in general these articles—commentaries and columns—fall into three categories: 1. Straight policy pieces (the welfare mess as described by authorities such as politicians or academics); 2. Policy pieces with a human touch (the welfare mess as seen by a case worker), and 3. Human interest pieces. The last tell a story that should touch a heart or funnybone or deepen one's insight into the world and its people. The Valentine's Day story falls into category three.

Above all, human interest stories are stories, that is they have beginnings, middles, and ends which together carry the characters, action, and, yes, plot forward. Although the beginning usually comes first in the chronological sequence of the action, it need not do so. The beginning is where the author chooses to start the story. It simply has to relate to and enrich the other key elements.

The beginning. If you have a story, know its major elements and how they fit together before you write the first word. Wherever you start, understand that the first words you write must be as organically connected to the story as your last ones. Remember, too, that these are the most important words you'll be writing. If the opening does not connect the reader with your story, it's over.

This one starts, of all places, in third-century Rome, with 249 words about the martyrdom of the historical St. Valentine. Note that along the way, the author finds room for a sentence playfully suggesting the emperor was doing his day's equivalent of tapping Valentine's phone and reading his e-mail. Resist, resist anachronistic excursions—for that matter any indulgence—just to show how clever you can be. None of this has anything to do with the story. Not only has the story's prime real estate been wasted, the author now has fewer than 540 words to tell the tale.

The middle. Next comes a rambling three-paragraph disquisition on Valentine's Day. The author dislikes designated observances such as Valentine's Day. This is a non sequitur, in other words, something that leads nowhere. He tells us how children are indoctrinated in the culture of card-giving in school. Love has more subtlety and depth to it than that, he informs us; and as grateful readers we say, thanks for sharing.

With those graphs and their 164 words, we are more than 400 words into the article. Some information and opinion have been offered, but nothing has related to his story. I have an image of the author feeding those words one by one into the Writer's Slot Machine, hoping that one of them will yield a jackpot. All he has to show for it, however, is that he has fewer than 320 words left to set the scene, introduce his characters, provide the action, and leave us with a memorable ending.

Do you see how a pointless beginning that is allowed to go on and on can leave you in an untenable situation? How a few graphs of this and that or whatever comes to mind are the prose equivalent of the time-wasting throat clearing a speaker does before ending the preliminaries and launching into the point of his remarks?

At last, nine graphs into the fourteen-graph commentary, we finally get to where the story begins: "A couple of years ago, I was talking and listening to a woman who works in an office down the hall from mine." It's simple and effective. Oh? the reader asks. What were they talking about? It turns out she is complaining about her former husband—no child support, little contact with the kids. He asks why she married him. So far, so good, but alas our author cannot handle success.

Before she can reply, he embarks upon an introduction to her response. The reader is alerted that "a masterpiece of lucidity" is on the way. A song should be written about her words. In just twelve words, she will pack angst, anger, insecurity, compromise, respect, and need. You can hardly wait, right? If you're lucky, maybe she'll follow those dozen words with the secret of life.

The punch line, the line around which he has constructed the entire piece, is short and to the point: "She looked directly at me, and in a calm voice, said, 'He was the first man to ever tell me he loved me.'" But note here: Even before she can get these few words off, he must interject himself again, lest we fail to grasp the significance of the moment. His introductory clause (*She looked directly at me and in a calm voice . . .*) instructs the reader to take what she says seriously.

Nor is this baroque embroidering done. Having let her have her one and only say, he must go on to make sure we have not missed anything: *She had covered it. . . . It was a history of love in twelve words. . . . She had sent along the great arrow of time to that moment in history when one human being first showed love for another.*

That is a hell of a way to treat a decent quote. A good quote needs to stand clear of any distractions. It is vulnerable to decoration and withers in the shadow of other words. It is its own attraction and cannot be improved by your commentary on it. *A history of love in twelve words.* When you make claims for a quote that cannot possibly be realized, you have done it no favor. Instead you've stuck a pin in it and the sound you hear is what life there was in it hissing out.

It is even a worse way to treat your readers. Have confidence that they can understand and appreciate the story at its best. Do not clutter your story with clues, instructions, and sly asides saying *Got that?* They do not move their lips as they read and they resent writing that treats them as if they did.

The ending. By now, with all the false starts and meanderings, the author has fewer than a hundred words for the ending. In the right hands, that is enough. In the right hands, the ending would have been planned before the first word was written. Let's see what we have here.

The author is stunned by the woman's twelve-word history of love. They look awkwardly at each other for what seems forever. Silence. Fifty-seven words to go.

As you write, you must always fasten in on what your words actually say, not what you mean for them to say or wish they say. The scene we are asked to imagine is bizarre. A man and a woman are struck speechless by what is actually a prosaic sentence. A lot of time passes. The sun is going down; the elevator is beginning to make noises.

He imagines that this sentence for the ages is actually visible before them, and suddenly curling out from the ends of the words, hanging in the air, he sees the bright image of her former husband, a halation, there between them, as if he were a fragment of a love song, once again offering love before taking it back.

Note that he uses the word "halation" to describe the image of the husband. It's an odd word here and telling, for a halation is the spreading of light beyond the normal boundaries of a photographic image. In other words, it reinforces the literal visual nature of the moment. We are intended to see all of this.

Who said you can't get high on words?

Now students, if I asked you to consider the various components of this commentary, from start to finish, and to write a one-sentence summary of the story, just what would you say? I'd be interested to see.

17

Keeping Control

After I read you the column about the walk our son Bennett and I took down Blue Springs Creek in Missouri, there was a question: Had I asked the boy if he minded that an article about him would be published in the *Post-Dispatch*? Yes, I had, and Bennett's concern was that he not be embarrassed by it.

He needn't have worried, of course, but that's beside the point. The issue raised is an important one for us as we explore column writing. In fact, there are a number of important issues for journalists to consider. When do they have an obligation to tell someone what he or she says will wind up in the paper? May your sources reasonably ask you to share with them what you wrote before publication? How much control over what appears in print are you prepared to cede to your source?

These are questions no journalist ever manages to avoid completely. Some may have hard-and-fast rules. Others may be more flexible. I place myself among the latter group, though I would hope that while my decisions may not always be consistent, my standards remain intact.

As you can see, we are moving into an area where journalistic decisions and ethical considerations are involved. Before we get into some specific cases, let me offer you a summary of my views of journalism and ethics.

For five or six years beginning in 1997, I moonlighted at Berkeley, at the Graduate School of Journalism. I taught the boot camp reporting course at Cal and some others, but my main assignment was teaching the ethics component of a required course called HEL: history, ethics and law. As an editor, I'd had a keen interest in ethical journalism (and how to produce it) and I'd served as the chair of the ethics committee of the American Society of Newspaper Editors.

I begin my discussion of ethics and journalism in newsrooms and classrooms alike by declaring that I do not believe in journalism ethics.

That's right. I don't believe in journalism ethics, that is, an ethics that pertains to journalism but not other endeavors of life. I believe strongly in ethical journalism but that is a very different thing.

I believe that the world is not divided into separate realms of ethics: journalism ethics, homemaker ethics, banking ethics, and so forth. We don't put on one set of ethical clothes to be journalists and go interview the mayor, another to be consumers at the supermarket, a third to be our children's parents. I believe there is one ethics that should govern all we do, an ethics that pertains to the butcher, the baker, the candlestick maker, and you and me.

Fundamentally, my philosophy comes from a conviction that journalism grows out of and is a part of life, rather (as some journalists seem to think) than that life is a part of journalism. A nice aspect of the way I believe is that you do not have to work hard to explain it to anyone. It works in college classes, in real newsrooms; it's worked wherever I've laid it down in the world.

Everyone understands it, because the ethics that should govern journalism are the very ones they learned by the time they were six years old: Tell the truth, minimize harm, treat people with respect, be fair, and so forth. Naturally, no one can do this all of the time, but if you go through life—and journalism or banking or whatever—trying to follow these rules, you will end up having lived an ethical life, which ought to be the point anyway.

The trick is how to reconcile these ethical values when a situation in journalism arises where two or more of our ethical principles are in conflict. Then you need to decide between or among the ethical values in tension—that of telling the truth, for example, against that of minimizing harm. Must every truth always be told? Must the risk of doing harm cause us to withhold important information from our readers?

To publish or not to publish? Often that's the wrong question. Ethics, I hold, is not a binary event: on-off, yes-no, black-white. Neither is life, for that matter. Doing ethical journalism is not just throwing a switch. It's trying to decide how to minimize harm while telling truth. It's trying to decide what to leave out, what to put in, where to play the story, whether to accompany it with a photograph, whether to put it in the paper tomorrow as is or hold it for further development or just kill the damned thing. It's trying to do the best journalism you can in a way that is respectful of ethical values.

Some editors believe that the identities of rape victims must be made public in the name of truth. Others believe that names should be withheld to minimize harm to the victim. Both sets of editors may be highly ethical. Ethical journalism does not mean that all stories on the subject must come out alike. What it does require—and mark this well, students—is that a process should occur by which the ethical issues and the journalism issues are considered before a decision is reached. The decision should be justifiable both on grounds of excellence in journalism and ethical sensibility.

If you think that's easy, let me tell you that I've never seen journalists wrestle with a tough ethical issue and then come out of the room giving each other high-fives. There can be satisfaction in it but there is rarely fun.

Now after all the heavy stuff, let's come back to Bennett Woo, who on the day of the column was just short of his tenth birthday. Bennett fell in the category of special people, who in addition to children include drunks or people high on dope, retarded people, those who are mentally ill, people who cannot speak or can barely speak the language, and others who may not be able to make good decisions in their own interests when a reporter comes calling.

They are especially vulnerable to exploitation, and the ethical principle of minimizing harm becomes important. In the case of Bennett, it required me to explain to him what I hoped he would do, remind him that I had never betrayed his deep feelings in previous columns, and assure him that this piece might educate people about something important.

For someone else I might have sought a surrogate decision-maker. Had he been someone else's child, I would have spoken to the parent. In the case of someone with language problems, I would have sought a translator. And so forth. The point is, when you're putting someone in the paper who is vulnerable, you seek an advocate or caregiver who can look out for the source's interests. That's not always a rewarding experience, but it's better than taking advantage of someone.

For a magazine, I once interviewed a woman who ran a street ministry in San Francisco's Tenderloin district. In addition to being the social justice minister of a large church, she was an accomplished mime and street performer, and often did her work in costume. She had saved lives and was justifiably a heroine to many people.

Years ago, when she was married and living in South Dakota, she learned that the mime Marcel Marceau was coming to Minneapolis. On that day, she took her kids to school, packed a backpack for herself with some clothes and books, left a note for her husband, and ran away from home.

Ultimately, she made her way to the Bay Area, attended a seminary in Berkeley, and got ordained. With a Catholic nun who had done street mission work in Central America, she started the project in the Tenderloin.

In the realm of contemporary morality, abandoning your children to fulfill your own life may run a spectrum from admirable through inappropriate to sinful. So in the course of our interview, I asked her, "Is there anything you do not want me to put in the story?"

I followed this immediately, however, by saying I would make the decision of what went into the story and what did not. But if there was something she felt strongly about and would like to make an argument to me for leaving it out, I would want to hear it. All she said was, please don't hurt my former husband; and that was easy enough. So, yes, I wrote of her abandoning her children. I hoped it helped readers understand the desperation in her life back then.

The control of the story should always remain with the journalist. But seeking information that can help you make a sounder ethical decision is not a sign of weakness or indecision. If you have faith and confidence in your judgment, you can take that risk. If you have an editor you trust with whom you can talk it over, even better.

18

The Importance of a Second Look

When you are assigned to a beat, it is important to maintain some independence, or distance, from it. It's easy to be captured by a beat and to assume that whatever officials tell you ought to go straight into the paper. That's especially so when the story is sensational and you have great access.

But there is never a moment when your critical thinking should be suspended, never a moment when it's enough to say, as a justification for printing something, that this is what the cops told me or the school officials told me or the "sources" at City Hall told me. There is no moratorium in journalism for checking it out yourself. Consider the story of Palestina Isa.

On an autumn day twenty-five years ago, Palestina, a sixteen-year-old Muslim girl, returned to her home in south St. Louis after her night shift at a fast-food restaurant. She and her parents lived in an apartment in what urbanologists call an ethnically changing neighborhood.

Back in the nineteenth century, it had been the home of German immigrants, who gave the area its name, Dutchtown. Then poor whites from the South moved in, and then blacks, and last came people from Asia, the Middle East, and Latin America. Newcomers to St. Louis, they found the sturdy brick apartments a good source of reasonable housing. The old-stock German Americans by then had long moved to St. Louis County.

Within minutes after she got home, Palestina Isa was dead, stabbed at least eight times by hand of her father. According to the account in the *Post-Dispatch*, the girl had demanded five thousand dollars from her parents and had then gone berserk.

Here was our lede:

Zein Hassa Isa explained Monday morning how some 12 hours earlier he took a knife away from his teen-age daughter and then plunged it into her chest.

"She came at me with the knife. If she not dead, I dead," said Isa.

There's no doubt in that account. He *explained how* he took the knife away from her. That she had a knife is assumed. As presented, that's beyond dispute and very different from, He *said* how he had taken the knife from her.

Explained tells us he was describing a reality. *Explained,* tells us *how* it happened, not *that* it happened.

In rhetoric, this is called begging the question, in which the conclusion is assumed from the premise. I've seen it in too many of your stories, and I want to say plainly, don't do it. Always be on guard against it when you write.

I remember the buzz at the morning news conferences when the city editors promoted the story for page 1A, where it ran the next day. We have this exclusive interview with the father. Terrific quotes! Enterprise!

The killing in self-defense was the police version of the incident, which we had in detail and which was not available to other media. The problem was, none of it was true.

As it happened, Martha Shirk, my wife, was suspicious the moment she read the story. She covered children's welfare issues and knew that violence in the home usually has a history. It rarely happens out of the blue. This, after all, was an A student in high school. So Martha checked with the child abuse officials. Her follow-up story ran two days later. On page 4C.

It turned out that there was a record of hot-line calls about the Isa family. People who knew Palestina said she was a "girl you'd be proud to have as your daughter." She showed up at school with bruises on her face.

We come now to a divergence of the definition of enterprise. The original interview with the father, Zein Hassa Isa, was described as a real scoop. It was an exclusive, though the story had come about because police had made Isa available to our police reporter. Working a beat, developing contacts, had resulted in a page one story. That's enterprise.

But Martha's piece was also enterprise. Nobody handed this one to a reporter. A beat reporter with sources had seen something that didn't ring true, and she had pursued it. I acknowledge a prejudice and personal interest here in the reporter, but I like the idea of journalists going beyond what official sources provide.

Unbelievably, here is what comes next. The father was suspected of being involved with the Palestine Liberation Front, and the feds had bugged the house. They recorded the killing and also other conversations.

Palestina Isa was going out with a black man. Her father was on tape saying his daughter was "a burned woman, a black whore, and there is no way to cleanse her except through the red color that cleanses her." To a caller, he had said, "Teaching her has to take place in the hotel under ground." In another conversation, he said, "I'll put a knife in her hand after she goes down, of course." Palestina Isa died in an honor killing.

The tape caught the terrible moments of the girl's death struggle. Eventually, her father and mother, who helped cover up the crime, were convicted of murdering their daughter.

Why am I telling you this? Because this is a story that repeats itself over and over. Remember when I mentioned Jack Lule's book *Daily News, Eternal Stories,* in which he argues that old myths and legends are the basis for the way many stories are framed, not just in literature but in journalism? Think of this as the story of the Ungrateful Child. Think of Lear and Goneril and Regan.

Last year, I read a story in the *New York Times* about a family in New Jersey that was arrested for starving some of its children. I may have a copy of it in my files and if you're interested I'll try to dig it out. The story in the *Times* was about a family in Collingswood, New Jersey. Raymond and Vanessa Jackson had taken in foster children, adopting some of them, and had two biological children of their own. Altogether eleven of them lived in the house.

A neighbor found one of the kids rooting around in a garbage can in the early hours of the morning and called police. The boy was nineteen years old and he weighed forty-five pounds. He and three other boys were removed from the house that day and the parents were arrested.

The lede in the *Times* said that police found that the "children, ages 9 to 19 had been starved." Note the past perfect tense. The verb form *had been* starved implies a deliberate act on someone's part. There's no doubt of it. The youth *was starving* is not the same thing. Somebody had done it to him. Later, the story quoted investigators as saying, "They ate wallboard and insulation to sate their hunger."

Law enforcement officials, children's welfare officials, the state administration quickly condemned not only the Jacksons but also the Division of Youth and Family Services that had been monitoring the family—as required when foster children are in a house. The press had a field day.

No one can argue that these children did not live in the most pathetic circumstances. Why didn't the agencies act? What kind of people were the parents? Who would be held accountable? This, in America?

The parents' protests were brushed aside. A report that the nineteen-year-old suffered from pica syndrome was pooh-poohed by officials. Pica syndrome is an eating disorder, characterized by ingesting things like plaster and paint chips. A statement from the family minister was ignored for a week as was a Web site created to offer the parents' side. It was too good a story. Think of Hansel and Gretel and the myth of the child abused by wicked adults.

But a week later, the *Times* published a long article declaring that "a more nuanced picture" had emerged. Ah. This one told of the savage infighting of social welfare agencies determined to discredit each other. Political issues were involved. Other children in the house were healthy. Something had gone dreadfully wrong, but it was not simple as the first stories painted it.

Before I wrap this up, let me mention very briefly another case, that of Richard Jewell, the security guard who discovered a pipe bomb in Atlanta's Olympic Centennial Park in 1996 shortly before it went off, killing one person and injuring more than one hundred. As you probably remember, the press did its best to convict Jewell of the crime. The *Atlanta Journal Constitution* put out an extra edition with this headline: "FBI Suspects Hero Guard May Have Planted Bomb."

Jewell, fat, unattractive, unappealing, was the object of a feeding frenzy in the media. Think of the myth of The Liar or The Pretender. As you may also remember, he was innocent: never arrested, never charged. The Justice Department formally exonerated him, something that it almost never does.

What these cases—Palestina Isa, the Jacksons, and Richard Jewell—have in common is that in all three the press enthusiastically, gleefully even, took the word of officials who were all too eager to place their own spin on events. In all three cases, journalists failed to exercise critical judgment and failed to observe the requirements of fairness.

If you cover a beat, it's easy and comfortable to look at the world from the point of view of your sources and to ignore their biases. Now and then a few journalists have the courage to say, wait a minute. Let's examine this more closely. I hope you'll be among them.

19

Our Changing Popular Culture

W hen I got home from Stanford last Monday, I said to Martha that I'd liked the line in the *Chronicle* that morning over a story about another milestone in world population. You remember, it was "And Baby Makes 6 Billion." Cute hed, she said. (No, that's not a misspelling; that's how newspaper people spell it, as in hed to kum, or HTK). Then I told her I'd brought it up in class and not one soul had gotten it—or was willing to acknowledge getting it.

The hed, as I told you, was a play on a famous line from a famous song. The song is "My Blue Heaven," and the line goes, "Just Molly and me, and baby makes three. We're happy in my blue heaven." The song was written by Harold Arlen, one of the best-known popular composers of his day, which lasted a long time. If you've seen *The Wizard of Oz*, you've heard his music. Surely you remember "Somewhere Over the Rainbow," which was sung by Judy Garland, and if that name doesn't ring a bell, I'm in deep trouble.

In any case, if you remember, in the same class I snorted at the use of "beer bong" in the *Mercury News*. That's beer bung, I said, the stopper or tap on a keg. And of course, I was wrong again. You all knew it as a device that shoots beer straight into the stomach, a kind of mainlining (to use a phrase that itself comes from another day) that trades the pleasure of beer-drinking for the effect.

In a way, this letter to you is about the great generational divide that is everywhere apparent. We the faculty in Communication got a reminder of this as school was beginning when one of the professors, Cliff Nass, sent around a list that each year the staff at Beloit College in Wisconsin assembles. The idea is to give teachers some clue as to what's in, and what's not in, the minds of the entering freshmen. Since we do have an entering freshman in our class, I thought you might be interested in some of the entries. Let's see if the people at Beloit got it right.

The list begins with the statement that the people who are starting college this fall were born in 1980 and goes on to say, among other things, that:

• Their lifetime has always included AIDS.

• Kansas, Chicago, Boston, America, and Alabama are places, not bands.

• They have no meaningful recollection of the Reagan era and did not know he had ever been shot.

• The compact disk was introduced when they were one year old.

• They were eleven when the Soviet Union broke apart and do not remember the Cold War.

• They are too young to remember the space shuttle blowing up.

• Tiananmen Square means nothing to them.

• Bottle caps have always been screw-off and plastic.

• They have never feared nuclear war. The Day After is a pill to them, not a movie.

• Atari predates them, as do vinyl albums. (And the expression, "you sound like a broken record," means nothing to them.)

• There has only been one Pope. They can only really remember one president.

If anyone wants the entire list, I'd be glad to send it on, but the point I want to make to you young journalists is how mistaken we often are when we think of what makes up our common popular culture—the events, people, products, performances, and so forth that we are likely to imagine evoke the same familiar response from just about everyone. (The recent showing of *Animal Farm* on television concluded with a shot of a couple, looking like Bill and Hillary, driving past in a convertible to the sound of "Blueberry Hill." The boys had watched it with me. "Fats Domino," I said to blank faces all around.)

You probably know of Silicon Valley's own Moore's Law that holds that the amount of data a microchip can hold doubles every eighteen months. There is a kind of Moore's Law at work in terms of popular culture. An entirely new universe of events, people, products, etc., is in place in a nanosecond of the world's time, and then just as quickly it disappears. It was not ever thus.

My American grandfather was born the year the Civil War ended, 1865, and he lived well into the 1950s. When he was young, people traveled by horse and buggy. When he died, Sputnik had gone up. (Sputnik was the Russian satellite that launched the space age. It went up on October 4, 1957, my twenty-first birthday.) The world changed tremendously in those years, yet the pace of change was glacial compared with what has come thereafter. What grandfather had to hold in mind to function in the popular culture (not Pop Culture!) of his ninety-some years was infinitely less than what you need to hold in mind—if you intend to be literate about the society around you.

So as you write, as you edit, you need to keep firmly before you with dead certainty that the metaphors and similes, the allusions and references, you use will be Terra Incognita to a sizable portion of your audience. They will read it with minds as blank as my sons' when I mentioned the great Fats Domino. What this means is that you must pick these allusions, metaphors, and the rest with great care. If you need to accompany them with a graceful word or phrase of explanation, do so. If your work is interesting, those clarifications won't hurt. What you must not do is ever write or edit self-indulgently or arrogantly. You may write poems or novels to please yourself, but you are doing journalism to convey information; and if the information is impenetrable or mystifying to your audience, you will have failed.

When I was a young reporter, I went to the federal penitentiary at Marion, Illinois, to interview an old prisoner who had been in jail longer than anyone else in America. He had murdered someone in the 1890s and had been sentenced to life. Now it was 1962 and in one of those acts of cruel mercy, if you'll pardon the oxymoron, the state was about to set him free. The old man, whose name was Honig, was terrified by the prospect. I asked him about his life in prison and he told me that one day, long, long ago, he had seen something strange and silver fly by overhead. It was an airplane. He had not known they existed, and he did not know how to go about asking what it was without seeming stupid.

As you do journalism, think of old Honig. There are many of him around, who will see something in your work that they never knew before and to admit it will make them feel stupid, or angry. Help them understand. The wise Henry Breitrose once said that journalists ought to be in making-sense business. He's absolutely right.

20

Attention to Detail

The *New York Times* today had a fine piece about the conserva-
tionist Aldo Leopold, and as I read it I thought back to the day
when a headline in the *Daily* was juxtaposed badly with a picture
of Governor Gray Davis, who looked sweaty as he gave a speech at Stanford. The hed was over a photo of a charity run, and it read, "Breaking a
Sweat."

Aldo Leopold was the author of *A Sand County Almanac,* one of the
classics in the literature of ecology, and in it he set out an ethical responsibility for people to respect nature. I'll try to connect the dots between Leopold and what we're about a little further on, but let me start
with the Davis picture.

That had to do with the editor's work in making the entire page come
together as a whole. Rarely in newspapers does that happen with perfect
harmony, but at the least editors need to keep the dissonance down, to
be alert to stories or photos or headlines that may be perfectly fine by
themselves but in proximity to another element on the page produce an
effect like fingernails on the blackboard.

Almost certainly, the person who placed the photo of Davis at the upper left was not the same person who wrote the hed over the picture of
the runners. A newspaper page is the work of many journalists, none of
whom may know exactly what everyone else is doing. The page editor
signs off on the final product and hence should have the same concern
for its quality that, say, an assembly-line supervisor has when it comes to
making sure a red car has red doors and fenders and not green ones.

An exculpatory thought needs to be introduced here, possibly to ex-
onerate our hapless *Daily* editor. Few things are more difficult to "read"
than how a color photograph will look in the paper. How a picture appears depends on many things: the quality of the color separation, the
register on the press, the mixture of inks, and exactly where in the press

run your copy of the paper is printed—early while the image is fresh or late when it has been beaten down on the offset blanket. From the photo in the newsroom, Gray Davis may not have looked sweaty at all.

The conscientious cabinetmaker or woodworker understands the concept of fit and finish and takes care and pride in ensuring that the whole table or desk is meticulously cut and assembled. A drawer that is a sixteenth of an inch from closing exactly on one side cannot leave the shop. I want you to apply the idea of fit and finish to your work.

Once, when journalists were trained by editors like Ray Lyle, that was routine in the trade, a word I use because that's what it was. (The journalists' union is the Newspaper Guild, and guilds were the organizations that grew up in the Middle Ages to enforce standards for trades and crafts. Not long ago, to its shame, the *Washington Post* led an effort in the courts to have journalists formally declared professionals. That's how lots of journalists like to think of themselves, but the *Post* did not have their self-esteem in mind. It was trying to circumvent the federal wage and hour laws under which professionals, unlike people in trade unions, do not have to be paid overtime.)

So in the larger picture, editors are there not only to keep the elements of the paper reasonably in tune with one another but to make sure that headlines or words don't appear that will distract, divert, or block the reader's attention from the main objective of the story. Sometimes, reporters deliberately inject such distractions.

The wickedly funny columnist Molly Ivins once was the *New York Times* correspondent in Denver. She wrote a story about a chicken processing factory, and in it she described how the hens were all "gang plucked" out in the yard. The volcanic editor of the *Times*, A. M. Rosenthal, went nuts and hauled Ivins in. You, he exploded, you wanted readers of the *New York Times* to think of the words "gang f****d." Ivins, ever cool, replied, Gee, Abe, nothing gets by you, does it? Shortly thereafter she left the *Times*, for fresh woods and pastures new, as Milton put it in another context.

In the smaller picture, in the confines of a single story, a single paragraph, a single sentence, the task of fit and finish falls upon the individual reporter or copy editor, who ought to take the same pride as the cabinetmaker in what leaves the shop. Fit and finish means clean copy. It means attention to detail. It means taking the time to use exactly the right word and not one just a degree off plumb. It means looking words up in the dictionary and usage in the AP stylebook; it means checking line-by-line that story in yesterday's paper instead of relying on memory.

In *A Sand County Almanac,* Aldo Leopold laid down the ethic of co-existing with nature like this:

> All ethics so far evolved rest upon a single premise: that the individual is a member of a community of interdependent parts. . . . The land ethic simply enlarges the boundaries of the community to include soils, waters, plants and animals, or collectively: the land. . . . In short, a land ethic changes the role of Homo sapiens from conqueror of the land-community to plain member and citizen of it. It implies respect for his fellow-members, and also respect for the community as such.

And that is how I want the dots to go together: for you to think of every word, sentence, and paragraph as a plain member and citizen of what you are writing or editing. A fancy word, a self-indulgent word, is a conqueror in your journalism's "land ethic." It requires the other members of the story-community, the other words and sentences, to be subservient. A wrong word, an inapt phrase, is a stranger in that land. In every story you write, you are creating a whole, not just some parts. In every story you edit, you are protecting and enhancing the community of words, that fragile domain over which you have been granted temporary stewardship.

21

The Uses of Introspection

When I came to Stanford in 1996, my new faculty colleagues urged me to be alert for the "teachable moment." That happens when something unexpected provides an opportunity to drive home a point you want to get across. Over the years, there have been a few of these teachable moments, but what I encounter far more frequently is what I think of as the learnable moment.

Perhaps it's selfish of me, since I benefit, but I prefer the latter, the learnable moment. Here's one from last week.

On Thursday, I began the day early with what has become a routine, every-few-months CT scan. These are relatively trouble-free events, the worst effect of which is that I have to drink a half-gallon of water afterwards before I can have a cup of coffee. There's a contrast dye they put in you that has to get flushed out.

The CT machine is a doughnut-like device and they slide you through it several times, taking detailed X-rays of the parts of the body they want to examine closely. A week later or so, I see my regular doctor and he gives me the results of the scan: progress, no progress, setback, whatever. Then we plan the next stage of treatment.

In any event, when I finished up, I went to the office and did the first-cut editing on your columns. First-cut editing is reading for pleasure and general impressions. I may make a pencil mark or two on the hard copy but that's all. Then, later, I move on to second-cut editing, which is the more detailed additions, deletions, comments, and so forth.

Around noon I went home for lunch with the intention of doing the second-cut work there. Martha was on the phone, listening to the answering machine, and there was an awful look on her face. Get right back to the Stanford hospital, the message said, and if I felt at all weak or short of breath, I was to go directly to the emergency room. The CT radiologist had found multiple blood clots in my lungs.

That, by the way, explains the awful coughing that you've had to endure the past few classes. I won't go into the details here other than to say the rest of the day was spent determining whether I had to be admitted to the hospital or whether the MD's thought the situation could be stabilized and resolved at home. In the end, I was sent home, but not before an evening training session in giving myself injections in the abdomen with a clot buster.

Many years ago, I was a medic in the Air Force, and I've told my family often of my experiences. Time to put your money where your mouth is, said Martha in tones ever soft and gentle. And of course, I have. Nothing to it, as people all over the world who have to do such things know. You can learn that. Your problems are the problems of millions of other people. Get over feeling special or picked on.

I've also discovered the source of my recent fatigue, though it scarcely ranks as a great moment in detection. When your lung function goes way down, as it does with clots, it takes more work to get the oxygen moving around. Between this paragraph and the last one lay a forty-five-minute nap.

If all this clot-busting stuff works as intended, the lungs ought to clear up in a few weeks, and I'll be back to normal. But that's not just a physical question for me now; it's also a metaphysical one. What I mean is, it's not just that I've never had this constellation of problems before; I've never been this old before. What's feeling normal for someone who'll be seventy in the fall? (What's normal for someone who's never been twenty-one before?) That's another learnable experience.

All right, you may be wondering by now: What's in this letter for me? What's in it for you is this. As you've probably figured out by now, this is a letter about introspection, about how to measure and describe ourselves when we find that life has placed us—as it does time and again—in situations we've never encountered before. I hope it will not surprise you to know that I believe the same tools and methods that we use to make sense of the reality we try to present our readers are the ones that are necessary here.

If, as Malcolm Muggeridge has asserted, the written word is fast becoming unnecessary, irrelevant, and obsolete, we journalists are probably to blame. To do our job properly, we need to be vitally interested in preserving the link between word and thought.

If we hold a thought in mind clearly and want to express it, not any old word will create that link. The need for the exact word to convey the precise meaning is what I've been driving at in all those comments on your papers about word usage. It is simply impossible to convey the right meaning with the wrong word. Missing it by an inch is better than missing it by a mile, but if you find yourself getting by with that inch, you'll be tempted to get by with a little more slippage.

To forge that link between word and thought, being precise in both is only half the battle. We now need to consider emphasis, tone, and what I think of as the architecture of writing—the what-goes-where part of a sentence or paragraph. If you want to describe your introspective reflections, the architecture of writing becomes essential.

Think of music. There, a B flat is a B flat, not a B sharp nor a C flat. It is a B flat whether you play it soft or loud. But in a passage of music, playing a B flat with enough force to shake the rafters and playing it almost inaudibly produce very different effects. Soft or loud have everything to do with the composer's conviction, which is also expressed in how and where it goes in the piece to create the desired effect.

There is no better example of this than Mozart. I think of him as the greatest of the composers, but no matter. He stands not only for conviction but also for the power of simplicity, which I've been trying to impress on you.

Before he became a playwright, George Bernard Shaw wrote music criticism for newspapers. Shaw, too, placed Mozart above all the rest, and he was scornful of those who thought his music no more than "tuneful little trifles fit only for persons of the simplest tastes." Mozart's music might sound simple, but there was nothing easy about it.

The most difficult writing can also be that which seems simplest and easiest. First it requires clear thinking. Next in the execution, it requires discipline. It is not at all hard to pile on adjectives and adverbs and subordinate clauses as if they were nothing more than the ketchup, mustard, relish, onions, and sauerkraut that goes on a hot dog.

This is Shaw on Mozart:

> In the ardent regions where all the rest are excited and vehement, Mozart alone is completely self-possessed: where they are clutching their bars with a grip of iron and forging them with Cyclopean blows [Shaw was thinking of Beethoven], his gentleness of touch never deserts him: he is considerate, economical, practical under the same pressure of inspiration that throws your Titan into convulsion.

What Shaw was praising in Mozart's music is what we should strive for in our writing: prose that is intelligent, expressive, and pleasing, set down in phrases that are perfectly clear and straightforward. Our aim is good journalism, Mozart's was art. In both, conviction is essential. We must believe in what we write; we must care about it. If we do not, why should readers?

At this stage of my life, I am trying to think clearly and simply. Somehow it seems more important than ever. Who would have thought that after all this time, it's still something you have to learn, over and over.

22

A Column Writer's Freedom

On my flight to the East Coast last week, I read a speech given back in the 1950s by the British curmudgeon Malcolm Muggeridge. Curmudgeons, as you know, take a habitually dim view of people and things. The word is classified by etymologists as "ooo" (of obscure origin), but some think it's derived from the Scottish *curmurring*, which means a source of grumbling. Muggeridge was a world-class grumbler. Even his name suggested it.

In this speech, he was saying that the written word was on its way to becoming unnecessary, irrelevant, and obsolete. "Over much of the world," he declared, "print has largely abolished thought." He went on to say that he did not see why watching television, in turn, would not abolish print.

Nonetheless, Muggeridge concluded his speech with an optimistic prediction. Television is so dismal, he said, that its cult would "rescue journalism from the triviality and sensationalisms which have so corrupted it in recent years." So far, at least, he has been proved spectacularly wrong. If anything, journalism is more trivial and sensational than ever. Which just goes to show that even when they try to be upbeat, curmudgeons just can't get it right. Something, I suppose, like trying to boogie if you ain't got rhythm.

I had gone to Georgetown University for its annual conference on language and linguistics. You could tell it was a proper academic meeting because our session was listed in the program as a colloquium instead of a panel discussion. The event was a hoot, as they say outside the ivy, and everyone had a terrific time. As one of the colloquists said afterward, we could have danced all night.

When my turn came, I mentioned Muggeridge and his speech. If the printed word is abolishing thought, it seemed to me, then we journalists bear a big share of the blame. Moreover, we ought to be vitally interested in preserving the link between word and thought. As I've said to you many times, unless we put thought into our writing, which is to say unless we think clearly before we write, what comes out the other end will be devoid of meaning. Our words will never enter the minds or spirits of our readers—or as Hamlet's prayer-challenged stepfather complained in another context, words without thoughts never to heaven go. (You've heard of GIGO in computerese: garbage in, garbage out. Now think of TITO: thoughtless in, thoughtless out!)

Now in journalism, of course, the product of words and thought are stories. As you also know, I'm concerned that when it comes to stories, increasingly journalists are paying more attention to the words than to the thoughts—at least to the rigorous thought necessary to capture as cleanly as possible a representation of reality, what my old editor Ray Lyle called "what happened" and what Walter Lippmann described as the lifting of facts out of darkness and assembling them into a picture of reality upon which people can act.

I had led Muggeridge into the discussion as a way of addressing one of the tasks that had been put before the panel, namely, to describe some of the changes we'd seen in how reporters approach writing a story. The change I mentioned, somewhat bleakly, was the trend for journalists to think of themselves as storytellers rather than reporters.

They are both taught and encouraged to think this way. Go to any seminar or conference on writing—like the National Writers Conference I spoke at a few weeks ago—and you'll find speeches and workshops on the power of narrative or telling great stories or even salvation through storytelling. (As Dave Barry says, I am not making this up.) People want stories, journalists are told. They want the great themes (love, death, redemption, loss) and they want heroes and heroines. When the Amtrak train went off a trestle near Mobile, Alabama, a few years ago, an out-of-town reporter, gathering information by phone, called the local paper and asked, which one's the hero? Every story has to have a hero. (I am not making this up, either.)

The trouble is, the world and its events are not usually amenable to our efforts to transform them into what literature students call the well-made short story, a narrative with a beginning, middle, and end. What is the "story" of the 1996 welfare law that took the federal government out of the business of administering the dole and turned the matter over to the states? Who knows? It may take a generation or two even to get to the "middle" of that story.

More and more, journalists are approaching such subjects anecdotally, though if we are honest we understand that we are writing only about fragments of existence, slices that begin after the beginning and end before the end. The new received wisdom is that if you tell the "story" of "real people," you will tell the story of the broader societal issue. ("Mary Jones stared out the window into the darkness. She moved heavily into the kitchen and put the coffee on. The kids were still sleeping. Five a.m. and another day. Once more, Mary looked through her purse, as if the act alone would put a few more dollars in it. Again, the rent was due. Welcome to welfare as we know it . . .")

Let me try to relate these things to what this class is about, the writing of opinion. You have been reading a lot of columns recently, and quite a few of them evoke the themes out of which much of literature is constructed—love, loss, death, and so forth. They are certainly narratives (perhaps David Broder's excepted) if not well-made stories.

But what sets some apart from others is the fact that they are manifestly crafted out of solid reporting. That gives the reader the sense that he or she is looking at reality, at what happened. If you read the Sacramento County coroner's autopsy of the Unabomber's victim, you would have found the very passages that Peter King used. (He was not making it up.) What King did was select certain parts of the report and integrate them word for word into his narrative. His columnist's objective was to elicit a specific moral response from the reader.

If you'd walked down Blue Springs Creek in Crawford County, Missouri, with Bennett Woo, you'd have made your way over the same chert gravel, in water just as cold and high as described, and you'd have seen dogwood, redbud, mullein, and all the other plants mentioned in the column. The author took the results of observation, interviews, and document research and tried to create out of them a narrative that would encourage readers to look at the landscape around them in a different way.

If you'd wandered into the nightmare from which Christie Blatchford constructed that complicated and textured description of the deaths by suffocation of three children who were playing in a trunk, you'd have found the parents, the firefighters, everyone, behaving just as she told it. There was too much detail, too much authenticity, too much of the product of the reporter's discipline, for her to have made it up. What gave the column its power was the way she organized the material (the fast cinematic cutting, for example—fade from the closed trunk at the instant of discovery, shift to the firefighters suddenly called into action) and the unexpected perspectives that jumped out suddenly. She had put the facts together to create a picture of reality upon which we could act, and by acting here I mean the coming to understand what happens at the death of innocents. You could see the world getting smaller.

Column writers are given an extraordinary grant of freedom. Unlike the reporter doing a straight news story, they need not tell us the who, what, when, where, and why all in a few sentences at the top. Unlike the editorial writer, they need not compress their information into paragraphs that are consistent with a particular form and tone, and they need not conclude with a message that conforms to an institutional view.

They can be as creative as they wish. A dry coroner's report, a creek in springtime, the desperate confusion of rescuers doomed to failure—all of these and more, whatever comes to mind as an interesting subject, are the palettes on which you mix the particular colors for your picture of reality.

As your reader, all that I ask is that it be interesting (or else I'd say to hell with it, were I not your teacher, as well) and that it both contain and transmit thought. All that I require as your reader is that it come as close to true as you can make it—that nothing has been invented or omitted or exaggerated or minimized so as to produce not what actually happened but what might have happened in the well-made story. And all that is needed to make this effective opinion writing is . . . you, the real and original you.

Do these things and I'll fight to the death any grumbling curmudgeon that comes your way.

23

The Parable of the Unhappy People

*H*ere's the scene: A swimming beach in the late afternoon. A child, let's say a ten-year-old boy, is missing. A couple of hours ago, someone saw him paddling out toward the diving platform. When his friends got ready to go home, he wasn't anywhere to be seen. They waited around for a while and then told the lifeguard.

Now the whole beach is hushed and apprehensive. Divers from the local scuba club are working the area and the EMS truck is in the parking lot, lights flashing, engine idling. Down by the water's edge and sick with worry are the boy's mother and father. And then suddenly a diver surfaces and yells something. He goes down again and the sheriff's deputies steer the little outboard over there. In a few minutes, they pull the body out. On the shore, one of the parents collapses.

The next scene takes place in the stricken family's living room. In addition to the parents, some friends and neighbors are there. On the mantle, there's a picture of the boy in his Little League uniform, the world's biggest smile on his face. Nobody can look at it without crying. Someone else is there, too, a reporter who's doing a story on the drowning for the next day's paper. That's you.

Perhaps some of you already have been there as a journalist. If you haven't and if you go into this business, chances are someday you'll find yourself in such a place. I have, more than once.

Now, in her devastation and misery, the mother looks at you and says, "Please don't put this in the paper. Danny was our whole life. It'll make it even worse to have to read about it. This isn't news. He was just a wonderful little boy and now he's gone." She starts to cry again, and when she is able to speak, she says, "I'm begging you. Don't make this a story."

You go back to your newsroom and tell all of this to your editor. What should the paper do?

The answer depends on who's being asked the question. That's what

Christine Urban, the social scientist and newspaper consultant from Sharon, Massachusetts, found when she posed the question as part of her survey on newspapers and credibility for the American Society of Newspaper Editors.

Seventy-five percent of the nonjournalists she interviewed said they'd respect the mother's wishes and not publish the story. The remaining 25 percent were split pretty evenly between those who'd run the piece and those who couldn't make up their minds. Seventy-five percent, though, is a clear, unambiguous statement. Loud and clear, the public says, keep the piece out of the paper.

Now for the journalists. What percentage would you imagine said they'd respect the mother's wishes? One percent. What percent would put the story in the paper? Ninety-three percent. The rest were undecided.

That's a stunning difference of opinion. An overwhelming percentage of the public is saying that it's either not news or if it is news, it's not important enough to override the request of a grieving mother who's just lost a son. Nine out of ten journalists say, ignore the mother's plea and put it in the paper.

Thoughtful journalists will say that how a paper treats the death of a child in such an accident can make a great difference. It can be done brutally or sensitively; but at bottom, publishing the story reflects a long-held view that a news organization's mission is to present an accurate record of significant events in its community—the bad along with the good, the sad along with the happy. And in most communities, the death of a child by drowning in a public place has some significance—or so most journalists would argue.

But the "news value" of the story is quite secondary to what I'm trying to get across to you here: that a vast gulf exists between what journalists think has to be written about and what their audience thinks should (or should not) go in the paper. In using this example, Chris Urban was telling ASNE that part of its credibility problem lies in the vastly different way that journalists and ordinary people look at the news. Both sides think that the other doesn't get it.

Alarmed by Urban's findings on this credibility gap, ASNE launched one of its biggest projects in recent years to repair the damage. The project focuses on accuracy, fairness (or bias), character (or ethics), and a lack of respect or familiarity with local communities.

For the past two years, eight selected papers across the country have been trying new approaches to these issues. The results of their efforts will be presented this year to the ASNE convention in Washington. The meeting that I attended at the *Sacramento Bee* a few weeks ago was to critique a handbook from ASNE that offers some solutions to the problems.

Shortly after Urban's report was released in the spring of 1999, ASNE asked me to write an article about it and the eight experiments that were under way. Each of them was aimed at a specific issue.

The *Mercury News*, for example, was concentrating on accuracy and was trying something called "prosecutorial editing," in which editors were to take a tougher approach to the framing and content of reporters' stories. *Florida Today* was working on factual errors and was trying out a new policy on corrections. The *Austin Statesman American* was focused on reconnecting to the community and was creating "audit panels" of readers who were convened to discuss bias in the paper. The *Colorado Springs Gazette* was also using audit panels to show whether there were significant differences in what the staff and the public thought was legitimate news.

None of this, I thought (then and now) was a bad idea. But I cautioned ASNE neither to expect too much nor too little from these initiatives. As I reflected about them, I began thinking of a story that you might call the Parable of the Unhappy People. Here's how the parable went.

Imagine a society where everyone once was fit. Now they all drink too much, they all smoke too much, and their diets are terrible. They are all under stress. Their faith no longer sustains them. They do not exercise. They rarely are at home. Their old friends are leaving them. They feel fat and lousy. They are all unhappy.

Little by little the awful evidence piles up. Utter ruin lies just ahead. Panicked, they commit themselves to better health. So one of them stops drinking to see if that makes him healthy, and one stops smoking to see what it does for her life. Each by each, they do something different: This person takes up yoga, another swears off McDonald's fries, a third starts jogging.

In a year they will meet to see how much healthier they are. What they will find, though, is that the one who stopped smoking but kept on drinking and eating those greasy fries and doing all the other bad things will still be unhealthy (and still unhappy). The same will hold true for the rest, for they are learning that good health is the accumulation of many smart habits. Unless you practice them all, you are unlikely to get back your old fit self.

That is why we should not expect too much from the eight papers' experiments. But what the unhappy people also will have found is that the one who stopped drinking not only felt better some of the time but also achieved a lower triglyceride level. The jogger lost some weight but also got a little cardiopulmonary benefit. They are discovering collateral benefits. So now the jogger sees the wisdom in living better across the board and stops drinking and smoking and eating junk food. Perhaps the next time we check, he will be measurably back on the way to health.

That is why we should not expect too little of the eight papers' experiments, either. They are likely to show us that small steps toward the restoration of credibility through the elimination of certain unhealthy practices (being casual about corrections, say) will produce positive results in ways that can be measured narrowly—and perhaps also yield collateral benefits. And just as quitting smoking is more important than doing yoga, some of the experiments will have deeper or wider benefits than others.

The trick is not to interpret these narrow findings too broadly. A paper that now has a better corrections policy may still suffer errors of grammar and spelling and will go on publishing dirty copy that readers notice.

Now the Parable of the Unhappy People, of course, grossly oversimplifies the problems that Chris Urban identified in close detail. And the solutions of the unhappy people are far simpler and less demanding than what the test papers are doing. *The Mercury News'* excursion into "prosecutorial editing" may have produced some real unhappiness on the staff.

Similarly, the *Colorado Springs Gazette's* examination of what readers think is news and what journalists think is news could well be wrenching for its newsroom. What will come of that particular experiment, I think, is that the public view of what's news will turn out to closely resemble the definition of news that once prevailed in newsrooms. If anyone reads the Urban report carefully, they'll find that the readers are saying that they want us to get back to the old ways—straight stuff, accuracy, good spelling, apple pie like Mom made.

Does any of this relate to opinion writing, which you and I are about just now? I think so. I think that just because we're writing editorials, commentaries, and columns, we're not immune from the problems Chris Urban identified.

If we don't care about accuracy and don't allow the facts to get in the way of our slam-bang rush to judgment, readers won't believe our conclusions. Our opinions will lack credibility.

If we don't know or care about the communities we write about, readers will put us down as out-of-touch and hence not to be taken seriously as commentators on local issues.

If we don't give consideration to the other side of the argument or to people with whom we disagree, readers will not be amused by our constant dissing and they'll put us down as biased and unfair.

And if we don't show a concern for ethics and decency, readers will disrespect us—just as we disrespect people without character. Which brings me to where I began, and the mother of the drowned boy, begging the reporter not to write the story.

Once again, you're the journalist. I'd be interested in knowing how you'd handle that situation.

24
Be Aware of Style

Four men stood outside the army recruiting office at Twelfth Street
and Grand Avenue at 7:45 o'clock this morning when the sergeant
opened up.

This sentence began a story that appeared on page 7 of the *Kansas City
Star* on April 18, 1918. It followed perfectly the requirements of the paper's stylebook, and it was written by an eighteen-year-old cub reporter
named Ernest Hemingway.

Style has always been taken seriously at the *Star*, and it was drilled into
Hemingway and every other reporter. It was Twelfth *Street*, Grand *Avenue*. The time was *7:45 o'clock this morning*. The stylebook confined the
use of a.m. and p.m. to timetables.

Hemingway never forgot the *Star's* stylebook. He talked about it in an
interview in 1940, the year he published *For Whom the Bell Tolls*. "Those
were the best rules I ever learned for the business of writing," he said. No
man with any talent, Hemingway went on to say, "can fail to write well if
he abides with them." (Note his classical use of abides *with* and not abides
by.)

When I was at the *Star* in the late 1950s, people still talked about a sen-
timental visit from Hemingway to his first paper. When he came into the
newsroom, he quoted from memory the twenty-word guide to good
writing that begins the *Star* stylebook: "Use short sentences. Use short
first paragraphs. Use vigorous English, not forgetting to strive for smooth-
ness. Be positive, not negative."

Hemingway also remembered this commandment from the stylebook: "Eliminate every superfluous word." From his writing, you can see
that he took it to heart. I wish all of you would, too. If you'd like to see
the words Hemingway learned to write by, you can find them in my old
faded copy of the *Star* stylebook, which I keep at my desk.

I thought of Hemingway and how newspaper style is worth taking seriously when a student confessed the other day that she didn't know how to use the AP stylebook. Worse, she didn't know *when* to use it. Let's see if I can help.

Why style? And by style, I mean here institutional rules of usage and not a manner of writing that distinguishes one author from another—Ernest Hemingway from William Faulkner, Tom Wolfe from Thomas Wolfe.

To begin with, virtually all nonfiction writing for publication is governed by some professional style.

When I was a graduate student in English literature, the handbook of the Modern Language Association was the gold standard for research papers. It remains so for scholarly writing in the humanities. Its purpose, as the foreword says, is "to introduce you to the customs of a community of writers who greatly value scrupulous scholarship and the careful documentation, or recording, of research."

The American Psychological Association's publications manual notes that its rules will allow writers to "express their opinions in a form and a style both accepted by and familiar to a broad, established readership in psychology." *The Chicago Manual of Style,* which began life more than one hundred years ago as a one-page guide to typographical fundamentals for writers at the University of Chicago, is probably the most widely used of them all.

As you can see, journalistic stylebooks are only a subset of a much larger genre. But whatever the usage—journalism, scholarly articles, business writing, and so forth—stylebooks and style manuals exist to bring standardization and consistency to texts. Their purpose is to dispel the chaos of every-writer-for-himself. It isn't, however, to impose a formula on writing, and now and then the requirements for following style should yield to a higher priority. The old *Kansas City Star* stylebook still says it best:

> The stylebook is not intended to set up a narrow pattern of writing or to discourage freshness and originality. Its purpose is to develop more readable stories by standardizing capitalization, abbreviation, punctuation, spelling, syntax and certain geographical usage.

Because of the reach of the Associated Press—it services more than seventeen hundred newspapers and five thousand radio and television stations in the United States alone—its stylebook has become the basic manual for American journalism. Imagine the difficulty a news organization would have if it tried to edit every AP dispatch to conform to its own style.

Even so, newspapers have their own styles that go beyond the AP and have their own manuals to supplement the AP's. For example, on second reference in the *New York Times*, the president is Mr. Bush. In AP style, he's just Bush. In the *Times*, the news agency is the A.P. For the AP (and for us), there are no periods between the letters.

For some specialized publications, the AP stylebook is clearly insufficient. The new AP stylebook devotes ten pages to the Internet, more than it ever had. The *Wired* stylebook, on the other hand, is nearly two hundred pages long.

Then of course there are peculiarities of style in certain news organizations. At the *Kansas City Star*, for example, there once was a high executive who suffered terribly from ophidiophobia—even reading the word "snake" was disabling. "Snake" was banned from the paper. You had to use a synonym. Reptile would do, but there are only so many times you can use the word, as one poor reporter found when a bunch of snakes got loose one day and caused a panic.

OK, let's move on to the how-to and when-to questions. We'll start with the simpler one: How to use the stylebook.

The first thing to note is that the AP stylebook takes the spelling and usage of *Webster's New World College Dictionary, Fourth Edition*, as its default standard. If you can't find something in the stylebook, go to Webster's.

Second, the stylebook is organized like a dictionary, alphabetically. It also is self-indexing, which means that entries are cross-referenced.

The stylebook begins with the prefix *a-* and ends with *ZIP code*. In addition to individual words, there are collective entries, such as *numerals*, which includes information about Roman numerals, Arabic numerals, large numbers, sentences starting with numerals, fractions, decimals, and a list of separate entries such as betting odds, course numbers, proportions, and serial numbers. If you can't find what you're looking for alphabetically, look for collective entries, such as organizations and institutions, possessives, second reference, and titles.

Third, there are special sections. I mentioned Internet usage. There are also ones on sports, business usage, and punctuation. Please make it your business to read the last. And of course, there's the fine briefing on libel.

Well and good, but when should you consult the stylebook? As they say in the Chicago precincts on election day, vote early and often.

That is, go to the stylebook the first time you have a title (like "Gov." or "Sen.") in your piece, the first time you wonder about capitalization (when to write "president" in upper case), the first time you need to use the name of a state and want to know whether and how to abbreviate it—you get the idea. How do you write the tabulation of votes or the caliber of a murder weapon? Is it "God" or "god"? What about obscenities? Is somebody playing "'possum," playing "possum," or playing "opossum"? In doubt? Check the stylebook. Use it early, use it often.

A good shortcut is the writing in newspapers, which has all been vetted for AP style. If it's "Gen." Wesley Clark in the *San Jose Mercury News* and "Gen." Wesley Clark in the *New York Times,* it shouldn't be "General" Wesley Clark in your copy.

In time, much of this becomes familiar or second nature to journalists and students, too. The need to look something up in the stylebook becomes less frequent. But it never goes away. In that sense, it is like the dictionary. If you write nonfiction for publication, whether in journalism or something else, you will have to be aware of style.

In the course of this letter to you, I have looked up AP style more than a dozen times. I also have been to the dictionary a lot. As I keep telling you, we need the latter more for familiar words than for exotic ones.

These are part of the writer's discipline. There's no way around it. And if you don't think it makes any difference, go to the Pulitzer Prize Web site and read some of the terrific stories there. Those writers managed to find time to check the stylebook. If they can, so can we.

25

Writing for the Ages

artha's been in New Zealand for the past two weeks, so I'm
home with Peter—the two of us, the big black dog, Webster,
and the two cats. There were fish in the pond until an egret
flew in from the Bay and ate every one.

Peter is sixteen. He has a really awful garage band, corrects me conde-
scendingly when I talk about almost anything, and thinks George Bush
is one swell fellow. When the president is on the TV, Peter says, "Good
man! Good man!"

His older brother, who's eighteen, takes it a step further. He wears a
New York Fire Department baseball hat and is a vociferous supporter of
Bush and his War on Terrorism. The eldest of the three, who's twenty-
one, attends a small liberal arts college. He complains that all the economics professors do is talk about why people are poor. They don't teach
you how to get rich.

Their mother and I cannot believe this.

Martha was an anti-war activist in the 1970s and editor of her college
paper at Swarthmore, a school founded by pacifist Quakers. Her professional commitment is to women and children in poverty. She writes
books about them. I edited the most liberal big-city paper in America.
People in St. Louis said we took our orders straight from the Kremlin. I
followed Joseph Pulitzer's commandment: *Never lack sympathy with the
poor.* So what's going on here?

Are these kids just rebelling against their parents? Perhaps. But I have
another suggestion, and it's connected to what I once heard Phil Bronstein, the executive editor of the *San Francisco Chronicle*, tell some young
journalists.

Someone asked him how the *Chronicle* was doing with young readers.
Terrible, he answered, and so is every other paper in America. As an old

editor myself, I know he's right. Is there something about youth that is turned off by journalism—at least mainline journalism?

For the connection between Bronstein's comment about journalism and our boys, I would direct you to a fascinating book called *Generations: The History of America's Future, 1584 to 2069.* Written by a couple of historians, William Strauss and Neil Howe, the book examines eighteen generations of Americans since the time of the Puritans.

Strauss and Howe discovered a startling pattern. Those eighteen generations contained four distinct peer personalities, and they have followed each other in exactly the same sequence. In four centuries, the authors found only one aberration, which occurred in the chaotic years after the Civil War.

They gave the four generational types names: Idealist, Reactive, Civic, and Adaptive. Each has a personality all its own, which it maintains as it moves through stages of life called Youth, Rising Adult, Midlife, and Elder. I'll get to Phil Bronstein and young people in a moment, but the key fact to bear in mind right now is that generational traits don't change as people get older.

A young Civic doesn't become a middle-aged Adaptive or Reactive. The judgmental righteousness of the Idealists, which took them to the streets for antiwar and civil rights protests in the 1960s and 1970s, didn't go away as they grew older. Instead, it made them the police force for political correctness.

Not every member of a generation exhibits the archetypal traits. Some, of course, may be wildly different from the majority. But in general, the generational personalities are these:

Idealist—In youth, attracted to self-discovery, turned off by team play. In rising adulthood, blurs distinctions between sex roles. In midlife, pessimistic about world affairs. As elders, preoccupied by moral principles. (Ralph Waldo Emerson, Gary Trudeau)

Reactive—In youth, desire for adventure. In rising adulthood, risk-prone. In midlife, a slowing down. As elders, uncomfortable with younger generations. (Paul Revere, Ernest Hemingway)

Civic—In youth, team players. In rising adulthood, draws distinctions between sexes. In midlife, optimistic. As elders, preoccupied with secular achievements. (John F. Kennedy, Ann Landers)

Adaptive—In youth, overprotected and suffocated. In rising adulthood, highly risk averse. In midlife, breaks away from conformity. As elders, most comfortable of the four. (Henry James, Sandra Day O'Connor)

Now where do we fit in? And how does this tie together our kids, Phil Bronstein, and the problems newspapers have with young readers? First let's locate ourselves.

If you were born after 1982, you belong to what the authors call the Millennials, a Civic generation. All three of our sons are part of it. Your parents really wanted you. You were part of the back-to-basics shift in education. In your time, *Time* magazine proclaimed the end of the sexual revolution. Your children's books were more about family virtues than family problems (Berenstain Bears). Mission-oriented, you'll finish the job.

If your birthday was between 1961 and 1981, you're part of the Thirteenth Generation, a Reactive. As the authors note, this was the first generation in America that women took pills *not* to have. It's the most incarcerated generation in American history and has a powerful, pragmatic sense of survival. It's bored with Woodstock and unsympathetic about people on welfare. They are America's greatest shoppers.

People born between 1943 and 1960, are Boomers, members of an Idealist generation and fixated on self. (The Me generation: SUV's, Botox.) The authors say that Boomers' preoccupation with themselves leads them to plan and judge on internalized standards, making them "better philosophers than scientists, better preachers than builders." Boomer women worried that marrying young and having a family might lower their standard of living. Again, self.

People my age are part of the Silent Generation, an Adaptive one. We're today's facilitators, masters of process over result. We've produced three decades of presidential assistants—but not a single president. We're America's only generation who, as polls show, would rather be part of another age bracket. We are Ralph Nader, Woody Allen, Bob Dylan.

Now remember I told you that the generations stay in type as they age. Hence, at any one time, there are several generational personalities active in America. Today there are five.

At the top are the vanishing GI generation (Civic), which ended the Great Depression, won a world war, rebuilt America. Behind them are my Silents, and next the Boomers, the Thirteeners, and last the Millennials, who are the new Civics. When we Silent Adaptives have left the stage, the Boomers will become the elders, the Thirteeners will be in midlife, Millennials will be rising adults and a new and as yet unnamed Adaptive generation will be the youth. As I said, the order of progression has held since the days of the Puritans.

Think of the effect of this progression on changing political attitudes, on changing social mores, on changing educational and spiritual values, on changing popular culture. As one set of midlifers, the most powerful political and economic age group, moves on to become elders, they are replaced by a cohort with an entirely different personality.

Parents often say, I can't understand these kids. When we were their age, we went to football games, dropped acid, joined the Peace Corps, respected our elders, whatever. Why can't they be like us? Martha, a Boomer, and I, a Silent, go nuts expecting our Millennial kids to behave as we did. The reason, of course, is that parents expect today's young people to be essentially like them when they were that age. They're not because parents and children come from fundamentally different generations. Idealist parents have Reactive kids, who in turn will have Civic children, and so on.

So here's the connection to newspapers and journalism. When I was editor of the *Post-Dispatch*, "cohort replacement" was the dominant theory about young readers. The idea was that in time and with exposure to the press, they'd becoming regular readers just like their parents. They would behave as their elders did. Research since then shows they aren't.

If idealist Boomer editors expect twenty-something Thirteeners to be readers with Boomer tastes and interests, they are in for a disappointment. The issues, the ideas, the visual presentations that appeal to the Boomers who put them in the paper may well leave Thirteeners cold—and older Silents saying the press has gone to hell.

As you write stories or commentary, you might think of your readers as a dynamic mix of generational attitudes instead of people just like you, though older or younger. What I mean is, diversity in journalism goes well beyond culture, color, and demographic characteristics. It also goes to the age groups above and below you that have distinct personalities of their own.

How journalists edit and write interestingly so as to appeal to an entire market of different generations is a terribly difficult question. It's more than an opening graph or a riveting conclusion. It requires a kind of smartness that I've never heard discussed in a newsroom—or a classroom, either.

26
Artists of Small Perfection

An obituary and an editorial tribute in the *New York Times* last week observed the death of Eleanor Gould Packard, who was as responsible as anyone for making the *New Yorker* what it is, the gold standard for magazine writing and editing. Yet, Miss Gould, as she was called at the *New Yorker,* neither wrote nor edited; neither did she check proofs for accuracy, nor did she polish. You might call her the keeper of the word.

For fifty-four years, said the obituary, Miss Gould "challenged the logic, syntax, grammar, flow, usage, punctuation and vocabulary of a legion of nonfiction writers"—among them E. B. White, John McPhee, and Lillian Ross. Hers were among the last hands and eyes to touch a manuscript. According to the *Times,* "she worked her way down both margins, penciling corrections and suggestions in a legible hand, always providing her rationale."

Of Miss Gould, it was said that her "great gift wasn't taking writers seriously. It was taking their words seriously." David Remnick, the *New Yorker*'s editor, said she was probably the only indispensable person at the magazine. And yet . . .

And yet, Roger Angell, a *New Yorker* writer and the stepson of the great E. B. White, had this to say. Yes, Miss Gould was a scrupulous reader whose comments had to be taken seriously. Even so, you had to know what to ignore. "If everything she recommended had been carried forward," he said, "it would be like the purest water—absolutely tasteless."

Angell was talking not only about the limits of perfection but also about the dangers of it. If all of Miss Gould's suggestions had been acted upon, the article would die. What remained would be a set of perfect sentences and paragraphs, devoid of color, devoid of taste, devoid of life itself. The attainment of perfection, paradoxically, guarantees failure.

This is a familiar theme in religion, myth, and literature. In the Garden of Eden, Adam and Eve achieve perfect wisdom but pay for it with their lives (and those of everyone thereafter, according to the Bible). Icarus, in Greek legend, soars to the heavens on wings of wax. Closer and closer to the sun he goes. Nearing the culmination of the perfect flight, his wings melt and he plunges to his death.

Perhaps you have read a poem by Robert Browning called "Andrea del Sarto." A High Renaissance artist, Andrea was known as "the faultless painter." Even if you have never read the poem, you may know some words from its most famous line: *Ah, but a man's reach should exceed his grasp, Or what's a heaven for?*

Michelangelo, Raphael, Leonardo—all, Andrea imagined, admired his perfect work, and perhaps they did. Browning is said to have relied on Vasari's *Lives of the Artists*. The fact, though, is that today few people today recognize the name Andrea del Sarto. But Browning's vision transcends the details of the nearly forgotten painter's art.

Though the faultless painter could render a line perfectly, could improve upon (or so he claimed) a drawing by Raphael, he could not bring life to his subjects. In lesser artists, lamented Andrea, there burned a truer light: *Their works drop groundward, but themselves, I know, Reach many a time a heaven that's shut to me . . .*

Religion, myth, literature—all warn that to approach perfection is death, one way or another. Sometimes it is by murder, as the many resurrection stories teach of figures that attain perfection: Baldur the Norse God; Osiris the Egyptian king; Jesus the Nazarene carpenter. Indeed, there are cultures where elaborate means are employed to prevent people from even attempting perfection. Moroccans, I have read, deliberately place mistakes of pattern into their rugs so that the weavers may not even seek perfection, which is the province of God, lest they blaspheme.

It is our glory or perversity as humans that we strive for perfection nonetheless, knowing its impossibility, aware or not of its cost. At one end of the spectrum, some use drugs and engage in eating disorders, which they think may lead to some perfect fulfillment of the body or spirit. The ascetic mortifies the flesh; the hermit turns a back on humanity. In renunciation, they seek a purer path. The compulsive and the obsessive attempt through doomed repetitions to attain through frenzy what they cannot achieve in study, reflection, good works.

What, though, has this to do with journalism? How can perfection and journalism coexist, even in the imagination? Perfection is eternal, but what can be more ephemeral than today's newspaper, last night's television report, the posting on the Web that is superseded in minutes if not seconds?

I have no trouble with the seemingly irreconcilable dualism of journalism and perfection. For I hold that what is perfect is made up of many smaller perfections. A perfect line contributes to a perfect drawing—if all the other lines are perfect. Should one part fall short, the whole fails as well. But in the imperfection of the whole, there may still lie treasures.

In the arts, for example, I find my perfection in small pieces—the farewell trio from the first act of Mozart's *Cosi Fan Tutte,* for example, or the opening lines from Keats's "Ode on a Grecian Urn": *Thou still unravish'd bride of quietness, Thou foster-child of Silence and slow Time . . .* Or Jess Stacy's long, building piano solo on Benny Goodman's "Sing, Sing, Sing."

I have no patience with journalists who fail to do journalism because they are paralyzed by the time, by the constraints, by whatever it is that they imagine prevents them from achieving perfection. Give me those who do their best with what they have under the conditions at hand. Sometimes these journalists become artists of small perfection.

I once heard a broadcast by the great Edward R. Murrow, reporting from London during the Nazi bombing. One night, he did a story on the quiet courage of ordinary people. When the sirens went off, Murrow stood outside an air raid shelter. Then he placed his microphone on the sidewalk. There it picked up the sound of the people walking. There was no running, no panic. Only the deliberate, unhurried footsteps of men, women, and children calmly getting out of the way of the bombs.

The best reporter who ever lived may have been the late Meyer Berger of the *New York Times.* In 1949, a deranged veteran named Howard Unruh calmly walked the Delaware River waterfront in Camden, New Jersey, and shot to death twelve people. On deadline, Berger retraced Unruh's steps and in a story rich with detail from observation and interviews produced what became perhaps the ultimate "from-here-to-there" piece of reporting. Once a prominent crime figure jumped to his death from a courthouse window. While other reporters were busy interviewing witnesses, Berger went to the window, climbed out on the ledge and took it all in—what he saw, what he could hear from the city below. Then he wrote what it was like in the dead man's last minute.

Sometimes perfection can be found in a single sentence, and when it is, it should be preserved, as perfectly as the scorpion preserved in amber at the American Museum of Natural History. Here's one, and it has a sting, too. It's also outrageous—as perfection can be.

In 1924, two highly intelligent, privileged young men, lovers named Nathan Leopold and Richard Loeb, kidnapped and murdered a boy named Bobby Franks. They stripped him naked and beat him to death with a chisel. They did it for the hell of it. The great lawyer Clarence Darrow got them life in prison instead of death. The two went to the Illinois state penitentiary at Joliet.

Leopold, a law student at the University of Chicago, was paroled years later. Loeb, who had been the youngest graduate from the University of Michigan, was murdered in prison after making advances toward another inmate.

In those days, anything went in Chicago journalism. The reporter who wrote the story for the *Daily News* was Edwin A. Lahey. He went on to become chief of the Knight Newspapers' Washington bureau. Some students of journalism say that his lead sentence about Loeb's murder is the best ever written under deadline.

The edition in which it ran has not survived, but according to legend, it went like this: *Richard Loeb, despite his erudition, today ended his sentence with a proposition.*

Miss Gould, the grammarian, might have chuckled. Whether it would even make the paper today in an era of greater sensitivities, no one can say. I rather doubt it. But in journalism, you take your perfections one at a time: a sentence, a story, a reporter's moment of genius. It's there; and if you come across it, remember it.

Part III

The Obligations of Journalism

27

The Three Pulitzers and Their Ideals

As a writer, I struggle constantly with discursiveness. In editorials, columns, news stories, magazine articles, even letters, I find myself constantly wandering, from this attractive thought, to that interesting figure of speech, to this wholly unexpected theme that suddenly lies before me, like a fabulous landscape revealed to the explorer: the Great Plains, the Rockies, the mighty Pacific. Stick to the beaten path? Not a chance.

More often than not, it gets me into trouble, as a similar itinerant trait led me astray in a little town in Croatia called Turanj, which lay between the Croat forces and the Serbs and was kept mostly quiet by some United Nations peacekeepers. Instead of staying with the story of the battle of Turanj, I saw an opportunity for a picture, of houses broken by war beside a meadow filled with tall green grass and white daisies. Yes, a photograph: the transient creations of man, eternal nature. As I went into the field, a little white cat crept by me . . . and if I could only get the cat in the photo, too. Before you know it, I was well into a live mine field and UN people were yelling at me and I was wondering how I'd make it back in one piece.

Writing can be a mine field, and if you go following the flowers and the little white cats and all the attractive images that come up, instead of tending to what you set out to do, you can find yourself wondering how to get back to where you need to be. Discursiveness, the quality of wandering in speech and written word, can have delightful results in essays, providing that the objects or sights along the way are themselves interesting and attractive. Life, after all, is rarely one straight line from here to there; and when people talk about the journey being more important than the destination, they are likely to be thinking of all the unexpected things they saw and learned along the way.

Letters are often treasures of discursiveness (and while I claim no treasure here for you, at least I can now take refuge in the letter-writer's grant to wander). They are not memorandums or assembly instructions doggedly written in an obscure tongue; they have the poet's license to see what lies beyond the next hill. How do I love thee? wrote Elizabeth Barrett Browning. Let me count the ways, and off her imagination went, wandering.

On the other hand, much writing needs to be disciplined. You have a story to tell, an editorial point to be got across. You need a dominant idea, a structure across which to build it. If you are skilled, you can do that job in a way that fulfills every requirement, including that of being interesting. If you are unskilled or undisciplined, you may see your editor looking at your copy with the exasperated expression of a parent thinking, I sent that boy to the store an hour ago for a pound of sugar and here he is, with potato chips, ice cream, dog treats, everything but sugar.

Discursiveness used to drive Joseph Pulitzer mad. The JP I'm talking about here was my boss, the grandson of the Founder, the Joseph Pulitzer the Great, the man who invented modern journalism and endowed the Columbia Journalism School and the Pulitzer Prizes. Many thought the first JP quite mad, but he's the author of that eighty-two-word marvel, the *Post-Dispatch* Platform, and had a powerful vision of journalism (most editors today would follow him across a sea of fire) and the words to give the vision life. Try this, from 1904:

> An able, disinterested, public-spirited press, with trained intelligence to know the right and courage to do it, can preserve that public virtue without which popular government is a sham and a mockery. A cynical, mercenary, demagogic press will produce in time a people as base as itself.

Hearing anything like that lately from Tony Ridder or Arthur Sulzberger or Dean Singleton? How about the chiefs at CNN or Fox or the networks?

From the Founder on down, all three Joseph Pulitzers were serious writers, though my Joseph, or Joe, may have tried his hand at something as frivolous as poetry now and then. He majored in art history at Harvard and bought his first impressionist painting, a Modigliani, when he was an undergraduate (laying the foundation for one of the world's great private collections). On Iwo Jima, as a young naval lieutenant, he came across a dead Japanese soldier whose kit held a sketch book, and the thought of a kindred soul dying in that bleak place never left him.

The first Joseph spoke in a voice of thunder. The second was more down to earth. He drank whiskey with his favorite editors and fistfights broke out at his duck-hunting lodge in Arkansas. Yet he never lost his focus and on his watch, the *Post-Dispatch* won five Pulitzer Prizes for public service, more than any other paper in the twentieth century—yes, including the *New York Times*. The third Joseph, my boss, never for a moment forgot that he was the custodian of a distinguished tradition. For him, the *Post-Dispatch* Platform, set down by his grandfather, was the crucible that he was fated never to set down.

In the early 1970s, he made me his editorial-page editor. Watergate came and Nixon went down; Vietnam fell; suddenly China beckoned. Was there a more glorious time to be an editorial writer? We went to China in 1976, at the tail end of the Cultural Revolution while Chairman Mao was still alive. Joe found the relics of the Middle Kingdom interesting and the food delicious; but otherwise China was hopelessly flawed. I was back where I was born, and it looked pretty good to me. When we returned home, he let it be known that he would enjoy being called the Chairman, which is how I addressed him ever after.

China was a place to go, but the Platform was a life's work, and together we went over it weekly, as if parsing the mysteries of holy script. Much of this hard work was done at a modest Chinese restaurant, the Shanghai Inn, which he liked because of the prices and its decent bar. Over drinks we would go over the words of his grandfather:

Never lack sympathy for the poor . . . How had the paper done this lately? Were there too many stories getting in about the rich and powerful?

Always oppose privilege classes . . . This would set him off on a story about one-upping the country club set.

Always be drastically independent . . . Alas, this meant that every now and then he would insist we endorse a Republican candidate. He didn't like it any more than I did, but the Platform commanded it.

And always there was this killer: *Never be afraid to attack wrong, whether by predatory plutocracy or predatory poverty* . . . We worried over this for hours. Attack wrong was clear enough and so was predatory plutocracy. But what in god's name was predatory poverty? The crisis came when he was to give a speech to the editorial-page staff and wanted to offer examples from the Platform. Everything was in place but predatory poverty.

Then a light came on. Mr. Chairman, I said, sitting down by his desk. Think of poverty as the predator, preying on the lives of the poor, the vulnerable, the innocent. Brilliant, I thought, but Joe Pulitzer shook his head sadly. No, he said. I think Grandfather meant the rabble.

Over the years, he taught me that principles mean nothing unless they can find expression in the journalism—or your life. It is the same with values. You can talk about them forever, write mission statements forever, but when the time comes to be drastically independent and you roll over, you have let down a tradition and sapped it of the life it needs to live.

I think of the Chairman nearly as much as I think of my own dead parents. Death lifted the chalice of the Platform from him, but by then it was as much my burden as his. And though I have left the *Post-Dispatch* far behind, I still think of those precepts and I think of how we worked at them, and I try still to give them life.

28

A Failure to Verify

As the sad story of Dan Rather and CBS unfolded mercilessly, I thought of an eminent white-haired scientist named Andrew C. Ivy, whose trial for fraud I covered many years ago in Chicago. I thought, too, of that humiliating night at the *Kansas City Times*, when after many failures to write a proper obituary, my editor Ray Lyle uttered the four most memorable words of instruction I have ever received as a journalist: Just write what happened.

Andrew Ivy was a physiologist and a vice president of the University of Illinois. Several of his students, as I recall, had won the Nobel Prize, though the honor had eluded him. How much that failure drove Ivy to his destruction one can only guess. I thought about it a lot as I watched the endless trial in 1965 and 1966—the longest until then in any federal criminal case.

Shortly after World War II, Ivy met a couple of slick operators from Yugoslavia, the Durovic brothers. They said they had discovered a cure for cancer, which they called Krebiozen. Did Ivy believe them? Who knows? But what happened is that he became their partner. Krebiozen was worthless, a substance drawn from horse blood without therapeutic powers. It did nothing to save lives. Ivy called a press conference to announce that cancer had been conquered.

The federal government indicted Ivy and the Durovics on charges of fraud and violations of Food and Drug Administration regulations. The prosecution went to exhaustive lengths but in the end, the defendants were acquitted. Subsequently, it turned out that the jury had been fixed. There were convictions of tampering and one of the jurors went to jail.

Like Andrew Ivy in the Krebiozen years, Dan Rather is in the twilight of a celebrated career. He is seventy-two years old, exactly Ivy's age in his time of trouble. Now nearing retirement, Rather had a sensational story—letters that purported to show that as a young Air National Guard flier, President Bush had shirked his military responsibilities and had received favored treatment because of his prominent father. Rather's scoop would have been the capstone of a career, much as Ivy may have imagined that Krebiozen would have been for him, had it brought the long-denied Nobel Prize.

The trouble was, both were fakes, the drug and the letters. Ivy is remembered as a quack. The reality that Rather offered was not the reality, in Walter Lippmann's words, upon which people could act. It was not "what happened." Instead it was a reality that Rather imagined had happened or wished had happened or pretended had happened.

I am not quite Rather's age, though I am old enough to hear, in the poet Andrew Marvell's phrase, time's winged chariot catching up with me. Three times I have been one of the three finalists for the Pulitzer Prize—in national reporting, foreign correspondence, and commentary. You could turn me into a trivia question about journalism: Who is the only reporter . . . So I know a bit of the aging journalist's dream of one last redeeming great story; and so, too, I have some sympathy for Rather.

But I also remember Mr. Lyle's commandment, and I hope if the time ever comes again and I am tempted that I shall honor it. I have not always done so.

At the *Kansas City Times,* you were supposed to write "verif." at the top of the first page of copy, right under your name. This meant that you had verified every fact in the story, and it was as close to a sacred trust as there was around the place. If you are serious about verification, it becomes part of you. Like a lot of other values of journalism, it turns into a way of life.

One day, after we'd come to California, Martha called to tell me she'd gotten word that a friend of mine from the *Post-Dispatch* was dying. His liver was gone from drinking and the doctors said he had maybe a day, maybe a week. He had been an unhappy man.

His wife had left him a few years previously, taking their daughter with her. She got the house, and he lived in a cheap apartment. He hated his work on the business page, and in truth he was no more than a marginal journalist. And, yes, I hired him.

I met him in Washington, the year I took a leave from running the editorial page to write from our bureau there. I was looking for an editorial writer, and my new friend seemed to be a promising candidate. He knew a lot about military affairs. He worked for a left-leaning defense think tank run by a retired carrier admiral, and that made him potentially a good fit for our liberal newspaper. He had some impressive clips from the Op-Ed page of the *New York Times*.

We used to meet after work at a place on Connecticut Avenue called Blackies. They had terrific martinis there, chilled to just above the freezing point and served in individual two-helping jugs.

On the basis of his clips from the *Times* and our good conversations, I offered him a job in St. Louis. He took it, and I was delighted to be bringing this nice, well-informed fellow to the *Post-Dispatch*.

Almost as an afterthought, I told myself that I really needed to check his references. So I called the admiral and asked about my friend's character, and it was sterling. I asked about his work ethic. Nobody at the think tank worked harder. Good, I said, because I've offered him the job. There was a silence on the line, and then the admiral said, "Ah, too bad. The thing is, Bill, he can't write."

And he couldn't. The *Times* clips had been heavily rewritten. He struggled as an editorial writer, and I labored to rescue his copy. Our union contract made it almost impossible to let anyone go after a six-month probationary period. I kept telling myself that with a little time and attention, his work would come around, but I was only kidding myself. So before you knew it, he was a permanent employee.

I felt terribly responsible for him, having brought him halfway across the country. He knew he was not doing well, and the awful expression on his face when he saw that his work once again was not good enough only made me feel worse. The mystery writer John D. MacDonald referred to that look as the one dogs wear in countries where they kick dogs, and if you've seen it once you'll know what he meant. That's how my friend looked.

When I became editor of the paper, my successors on the editorial page wrestled with his copy, and finally one of them said to hell with it and shipped him off to the business page. People at the paper who talked to me after I left for California said he was coming to work drunk. And then, a few days after we heard that he was dying, the systems finally all shut down, and he was gone.

I often wonder what would have happened to my friend had he never left the security of the think tank and tried to swim in waters that were too deep and too fast for him. He was, of course, responsible for his own life and what he made of it. And yet, thinking of him now, I wonder if things might have been different if I had done what Mr. Lyle had tried to teach me long ago.

I neglected process. I did not do the things that are necessary to respect the reality that is. Instead, I acted upon the reality that I imagined or that I wanted—in the way that too many journalists do to avoid the hard work that may compel them, if they are honest, to scrap everything and start over from the beginning. I took things on face value and I did not verify, and although there is no straight unbroken line from there to here, I wish very much that I had it all to do over again.

29
Read, Read, Read

Clay Haswell and I go back a ways, and I respect him a lot. Clay and I have some similar experiences, such as getting sideways with the owners of our newspapers. More important, we share a view of what you might call the moral life of journalists.

We met at the Rand Corporation in Santa Monica sometime back in the 1980s, when Clay was editor of the *Contra Costa Times* and I was at the *Post-Dispatch*. A nonprofit called New Directions for News organized a meeting at Rand, which began after World War II as an Air Force think tank and then branched out into other areas.

The meeting had a grandiose purpose, to revolutionize journalism by creating new forms, new approaches, and so forth. I suspect both Clay and I were in the wrong place. My view is that revolutions are created by inspirational or visionary individuals, not by committees working on prototypes of front pages. In any event, over the years we stayed in touch.

As I'm sure he told you, when Clay took the job with AP in San Francisco, he said he'd only do it if he could continue helping journalists in places where a free press is only a remote ideal. Doing that was more important to him than whether the AP would hire him. It was a moral decision.

I do a little of that work myself, in China mostly, but also elsewhere in Asia and, for the last two years, in Montenegro, where I'm helping journalists sort out the problems of self-regulation. Clay goes to grittier places, but both of us know that the people we work with face problems American journalists rarely encounter. That's one of the things you consider—that just by talking to you, someone's livelihood may be taken away or that a good man or woman may wind up in a dark, damp place and nobody may know where they are for a long time.

I began to seriously reflect on the moral life of journalists some years ago, when I thought of writing a book about my childhood. I was a boy of two races, of two countries, of two cultures, of a broken home, raised by a single parent. I had lived through a war, through occupation by the enemy. I wondered if these conditions—ones not unfamiliar to many children—helped shaped a particular outlook on the world and its possibilities.

I wrote to Robert Coles, the Harvard psychologist. He was immediately encouraging and sent me one of his books, *The Moral Life of Children*. The book grew out of his experiences with a little girl who had been one of the children to integrate the New Orleans school system. She had been reviled, cursed, and threatened. Yet she kept her moral center. She forgave those who hated her. She stayed sane.

I began thinking of a dilemma many journalists face. We often confront problems that pull us in different directions, toward journalism and its canons, toward doing whatever we can to help bring light to people who live in darkness. How can we compose these impulses? How can reporters and editors remain sane and on a moral center?

A few years ago, a student wrote saying that reading newspapers—as I had required of her class—had been a great help. What else could I suggest? It may come as no surprise to you that I had nothing else to offer. The thing to do, I said, "is to read, read, read."

When I wrote her, and behind everything I say to you, I have in mind John Donne, the seventeenth-century poet. In 1623, not long before he died, Donne wrote a set of devotions.

By far the best-known lines from these are the ones that say, "No man is an island, entire of itself; every man is a piece of the continent, a part of the main; if a clod be washed away by the sea, Europe is the less . . . " And then come the words that still retain the power to send a chill through us: "any man's death diminishes me, because I am involved in mankind, and therefore never send to know for whom the bell tolls; it tolls for thee."

And that is the point of "read, read, read." Newspaper editors and marketers prattle about being "connected to readers." But what I say to you is that none of us as journalists will ever be connected if we are not involved in mankind, if what happens in Belarus or Thailand or East Palo Alto is not important to us.

If we do not know what is happening, if we are indifferent to that great continent of humankind, we shall never report or write other than superficially. The questions of the moral life of journalists will be irrelevant for us.

Once a black South African journalist named Rehana Rossouw came into my ethics class at Berkeley. She told us how in covering the atrocities of apartheid her paper never printed the explanations of the police. There was only one truth. To present another side of the story would only detract from the transcending moral duty to oppose apartheid.

She believed that the accepted rules for journalism had to be suspended in South Africa. Some in the class were taken aback by this.

Yet the ethicist Sissela Bok might agree. If the survival of society itself is at stake, she wrote, one lie for a good cause may not matter so much. So I wondered if for journalism, when society's very survival is at risk, as it was for black South Africans during apartheid, conduct that otherwise would be unethical might be condoned. I haven't worked that out yet.

A little later, we heard from Orville Schell, the dean of the Graduate School of Journalism at Berkeley. Orville is a specialist on China and also a director of Human Rights Watch. He helped smuggle cameras into Chinese jails for a *60 Minutes* exposé of how China profits from the sale of goods produced by prisoners who labor under inhumane conditions.

I asked him how he was able to reconcile journalism and his activism on behalf of oppressed people. He answered simply, "I believe I am my brother's keeper."

Those words are from one of the most famous passages in the Bible. In the book's first homicide, the two sons of Adam and Eve quarrel and one of them, Cain, kills the other, Abel. Cain feigns ignorance when God asks him where Abel is. "Am I my brother's keeper?" he says.

Ever since, the question has posed a central moral problem: Are we responsible for the welfare of our fellow human beings? Orville Schell answers Yes. So, I would say, do the journalists Rehana Rossouw and Clay Haswell. They hear the tolling of the bell. But what about you? What about me?

These are questions that we answer in the privacy of our own hearts. But if we also answer affirmatively, what is the implication for the journalism we do? Orville Schell's answer, and mine, is that it must be done honestly—that the facts must be true, that the presentation must be scrupulous—and importantly that we do not damage journalism in the process.

These are not easy choices. If you read widely, you are more likely to become engaged in a worthy cause. Honorable journalists have been able to balance their causes with their profession, though their conduct may leave them open to questions and criticism. Other honorable journalists have not—and one or the other, their cause or their journalism, falls by the wayside.

In discussing with you the moral life of journalists, my aim is not to direct you in one direction or another. It is—and you may not thank me for it—to encourage you to confront hard choices. It is those choices, the hard and not the easy ones, that keep us sane in the long run. Clay Haswell is a sane man. And I believe that learning to put ourselves in the way of difficult decisions is the purpose of an education—and certainly the one I want to provide you.

30
The Importance of Character

A s I'm editing your stories, I imagine you out there awaiting the
results with feelings less of anticipation than of resignation. One
of you once wrote me, saying, "I am also fully expecting to receive
a sea of red of Bolshevik proportions appear in my inbox."

All those red or blue words and strike-throughs. All those highlighted
boxes.

Follow AP style. Use the dictionary. Two words not three. One word,
not two. Move that subordinate clause so subjects and verbs don't have
long-distance relationships. Get that attribution high in the quote. At-
tribute this fact. Avoid redundancies. How do we know this? More clutter. Another reference to that damned Ray Lyle.

What the hell is going on? Did I go to journalism school for *this?*

If you're like the other students I've known here and at Berkeley, you
didn't decide to get that MA so you could memorize the AP stylebook or
write a summary lede in your sleep. No, there was something larger. You
wanted to be a foreign correspondent, do investigative reporting, write
long-form stories. You had an ideal; you wanted to make a difference.
And to all of these things, I say, good for you, good for journalism.

I would fail as your teacher, and I would fail myself, if I did not do all
I could to show you the larger purpose to our endeavor, the public mission that good journalism serves, the possibilities that lie before us if only
we grasp them. I would fail if I didn't let you know how much I believe
that there is still nobility in what we're about, despite our many self-
inflicted wounds and the shabby execution that we see in the media all
around us.

But I would fail equally if I did not help you understand that the con-
summate professionalism toward which we all strive, which you will
need to succeed, at bottom is an accumulation of small, homely habits

that we reinforce every day. All of this is to introduce you to someone you'll never know.

His name was Bob Pearman and he died of cancer about two years ago. Bob was a reporter at the old *Kansas City Times* and later he was the editor of the *Omaha World-Herald*. But long before that, he was just another scared Marine second lieutenant stuck on a hilltop in Korea. I'll begin my story about him there.

On this late afternoon, a North Korean attack was expected, and Pearman's platoon was badly outnumbered. They had orders to hold the hill. Pearman was a country boy from the Dismal River country, out in western Nebraska where the nearest towns are seventy miles away, and he had learned to take his chores seriously. So on this day in Korea, he'd done what needed to be done.

He had his troops dug in near some bunkers. He had put out his patrols. His perimeter defenses were in order, and with all that finished, he settled in to wait—and probably to die. As night fell, the attack came.

It was too dark for air cover and the artillery was not stopping the North Koreans. The patrols withdrew. The perimeter held for a while and then was breached. He and his men fired as fast as they could, nearly point blank. And so finally there was only one thing left for them to do.

The young lieutenant ordered his men into a bunker and they buttoned the thing up as best they could. Then Pearman called in the American artillery—with instructions to put the high-explosive shells directly on top of their own position. They might be killed, but so would the attackers. Perhaps the hill could be saved.

Miraculously, the desperation tactic worked. The enemy was driven back. The platoon emerged alive.

After the war, Pearman decided to become a reporter, and he went to the journalism school at Columbia, where he won the Silurian Award as the best reporter there. His first job was as a copy boy on the *New York Mirror*, a second-rate paper that folded long ago, and after that he got on at the *Kansas City Times* and became another of Ray Lyle's boys. I think of him every time I tell my students that I want them to do the simple, fundamental things over and over and over.

What made Bob Pearman a good journalist was his skill, his intelligence, his talents. What made him one of the best I've ever known was his character. There were some reporters who were better writers. There were those who knew more about their subjects. There were those with superior sources. But there was not one I've ever met who worked harder, who paid more attention to small and humble details, who kept focused longer.

He became a good writer by writing and writing and writing and learning from his mistakes. I can still see him at his desk late at night, reworking some freelance story about the Dismal River country that he hoped to sell somewhere. We were all short of money then, but Bob, who was a little older than the rest of us, had a wife and small boy.

Pearman never quit on an assignment—or anything else. He never lay down on his editors. He took responsibility. It was very easy for me to see in this colleague the younger man who had pulled the bunker door shut and called down the artillery.

I suppose that he learned much of this out along the Dismal River in Nebraska, where people pull their own weight or fall by the wayside, where chores undone mean dead livestock and where 5 a.m. is always dark and cold. Out where there's nothing around but your own voice in your head, telling you to do that tedious job one more time for the simple reason that it hasn't been done right yet.

There are a million miles, in a way, between that place and our Stanford classroom, here in the heart of Silicon Valley where brilliance is all around and miracles of high technology are taken for granted. Perhaps here it sounds quaint to hear someone say that there is an essential connection between success and simple repetitive tasks, done so many times that they become unbreakable habits that will last a lifetime.

And yet the good writers pay attention to every comma. The good reporters verify a brief as if they were working on a Pulitzer Prize story. Over and over, the good musicians play the same do, re, mi's that children do. It is said that the great cellist Pablo Casals practiced his scales on the day he died—as he did every morning of his life.

Bob Pearman did well enough in journalism to buy a farm and raise racehorses—the sort of retirement life that Silicon Valley types might aspire to. Bob didn't get there overnight, of course. He did it the old-fashioned way he had been taught: one step at a time. The way I'm trying to teach you.

31
Children and War

*T*his letter is about children and war. It is also about journalism. When I wore the Air Force uniform many years ago, I did not come under enemy fire. I was just a medical corpsman and I flew around the country in airplanes with a big red cross on the tail. We took care of a few wounded servicemen from Vietnam, but this was before the big American buildup there.

But many years earlier, as a small boy, I lived in a city where bombs fell and where war was part of everyday life. I must confess that the experience was often exhilarating. I did not know any better. I have tried to remember my reactions to the noise and the sights of war and I have tried to imagine what the children of Afghanistan are living through.

It is difficult to know the extent to which children are suffering from the attacks upon Afghanistan. The Taliban says civilian casualties number two hundred or three hundred. If true, that is a fraction of the number of the people killed in the terrorism against the United States, so we need also to think of the effect of the war on American children who have suffered unimaginable losses of their own.

As to the bombing of Afghanistan, the United States declares that it is exercising extreme caution to avoid civilian casualties. I have no reason whatsoever to doubt this. Even so, people are dying.

The *New York Times* reported today on the death and destruction that a credible journalist had seen in a town called Karam, which was destroyed by bombing. What is certain is that over the years, the children of Afghanistan have been profoundly affected by war. Human Rights Watch declares that in the past twenty years, some 1.5 millions Afghans have died as a result of fighting in that country.

As we consider children and war, we need first to distinguish among three kinds of them. They have different experiences, but all are affected by media. What we do as journalists matters to them all.

First, there are the children in war zones for whom the action is essentially theater. These are the children who see war first-hand but from a distance, from safe ground.

Once, I was one of them. Yet the fact that these more fortunate children may escape the immediate ravages of war does not mean that the violence leaves no mark upon them, that scar tissue does not form upon their souls. Though these children are on the sidelines of war, they are touched daily by media—what the radio is saying or what appears in the newspapers or on television.

Are terrifying rumors being spread? What is the depiction of the enemy? Are these children being taught to hate where yesterday they had no such feelings? Almost certainly, the answer is, Yes. And almost certainly, too, we the media are among the most effective propagators of these terrible lessons.

The second kind of children are those who are personally scorched by war. In the most immediate, unmistakable sense, these are victims. Within my lifetime, there have been two searing media images of such children.

One was a photograph of a baby, a refugee, sitting all alone and crying in the bombed ruins of the north railroad station in Shanghai. This was in 1937. The photographer had the improbable name of Newsreel Wong and is a legend in Chinese photojournalism. Wong's picture went all around the world and many people for the first time understood the effect of that war on civilians.

The other was a picture of a naked young girl running hysterically down a road in South Vietnam, her clothing burned off by napalm. Perhaps you have seen this one.

The photograph was among those images which were instrumental in creating the public indignation that ultimately forced the war to be stopped. These were pictures taken by journalists recording the war, and the government readily understood their effect on public opinion. Many generals and politicians considered the press disloyal.

Through the images of their misery, these children attained a kind of immortality; and through journalism, they touched the conscience of the world. That was something no government could stop.

For children of this second kind, war is never an excitement or a glory. Orphaned, maimed, disfigured, traumatized, they carry with them all their lives the effects of war. They are the flesh-and-blood representations of the abstractions of politicians and generals and terrorists, the results of the surgical bombing, precision anti-aircraft suppression, or strikes against civilians in retaliation for this or that past injustice. And since no neighborhood anywhere is without children, inevitably there already are some of these children in Afghanistan.

The third kind of children are those touched most of all by media. Many of them live today in the United States but they can be found elsewhere as well. For these boys and girls, the threat of war or violence by bombs, sabotage, and the rest have suddenly become real because of what they have seen and read in the media. They will remember September 11, 2001, as long as they live.

They bear no physical signs of war or terrorism and most are likely to go on to lead the outward lives of normal men and women. But inside, in places they may never realize, these children have been touched by the violence, and something has happened to the world as they imagined or understood it to be.

One crucial condition, however, binds all three kinds of children. That is their utter helplessness. From the perspective of the child in war, every event lies far beyond his or her powers of influence. The child lives in ignorance, unaware or uncomprehending of the reasons for the surrounding violence. And, hence, the child is both constantly surprised by what is taking place and constantly apprehensive of what may suddenly happen.

For even the fortunate child in war, there can be no security, no stability, no sense of assurance that the small part of the world that is his or hers is under control. The child may thrill, as I did, to distant smoke columns and the sight of airplanes wheeling in the sky, but long afterward the sound of a siren in the night will produce a terror that the child may never fully understand or escape.

For the child in war, the sense of powerlessness is crushing and enduring. For the child in war, the world very early on becomes a place that can never be fully trusted. An acute awareness of vulnerability is a condition of life: better, for such a child, not to give too much of one's self.

Like the children of Afghanistan, the boys and girls of America are also experiencing a war. We should be grateful that the vast majority of them will remain witnesses from a great distance, although some children already are suffering the incurable grief that follows the death of a parent or relative—in New York or Washington or in a field in Pennsylvania.

Like their unfortunate counterparts in loss in Afghanistan, an effect of war will always be part of them.

If we are not careful, however, a subtler part of war will be left upon the children for whom the battle is no closer than the television. There are honorable arguments for and against this war that the United States is now prosecuting. So as the conflict proceeds, it is profoundly important, I think, for the media to present events with proportionality, neither exaggerating nor trivializing them or the political forces that brought them about.

We journalists instruct the children's most important teachers, who are their parents. This is not the World Series or a video game or a fight over a parking space. We are not protecting our children's sensibilities if we allow them to regard war in this way, which they will surely do if that is how we in the media present what is happening.

We do our children no favor by encouraging in them an indifference to sacrifice and suffering. We do them no favor by encouraging them to view people in distant lands—or their neighbors—with suspicion or hostility. And if we the media do those things, we also do no favor to America, which has suffered in a way that it has never suffered before.

32

A Case of Libel

About twenty miles upstream from St. Louis on the Mississippi River lies the historic town of Alton, Illinois. There in the summer of 1980, a journalist's nightmare occurred.

Alton was established by French fur traders in a place that much later became Madison County. Four miles south is the great junction of the Missouri and Mississippi rivers. From this meeting of the waters, Lewis and Clark set off on their exploration of the trans-Mississippi West.

Here in 1837, Elijah Parish Lovejoy, the abolitionist preacher and publisher, became America's first journalist martyr when a pro-slavery mob murdered him and then threw his presses into the river. Here in 1858, Abraham Lincoln and Stephen Douglas held the last of their famous debates about slavery.

And here for more than 150 years was published a newspaper called the *Alton Telegraph*. By 1980, the paper had a circulation of some thirty-eight thousand. It was family-owned and proud. Not many papers could say that Abraham Lincoln had appeared in local news articles.

Our story begins with a prominent apartment developer named James C. Green. As a big-time builder, he needed a large and ready line of credit. In the late 1960s, Green's activities and the rumors around them came to the attention of two investigative reporters for the *Telegraph*.

They were looking into possible Mafia connections in Madison County. A federal anti-crime strike force had been formed, and it also was investigating. The reporters developed information that mob money was being funneled into the Piasa First Savings and Loan Association, which in turn was lending money to Green.

The reporters surmised that Green was involved with the Mafia. That might explain the mob's investments in Piasa. The money lent by the S&L to Green could be illegal kickbacks, in which case he was a racketeer.

The reporters got some leads from the sheriff's office and elsewhere but the investigation bogged down. So in 1969, they wrote a confidential memorandum to the federal strike force, alleging that Mafia money was going into Piasa.

In the memo, they accused Green by name of receiving kickbacks and said he was associated with "hoods." The reporters asserted that Green had a silent partner who was "the No. 2 crime boss in the county." The reporters asked the strike force to verify this information.

It was explosive stuff. The trouble was, nothing came of it.

The reporters' work eventually ran into a dead end. They could find no wrongdoing by Green or Piasa. The tip to the feds produced nothing. There was no story. The paper did not publish anything. The project went onto hibernation.

But if the journalists came up empty-handed, the roof was falling in on James C. Green. His financing dried up. His contracting business failed. He found himself financially destroyed and he did not know why. This mega-developer, who had put up twenty-five hundred apartment units, now worked as a common carpenter.

What had happened was this. Though the federal strike force decided against a criminal investigation of Green, it nonetheless sent the details of the reporters' memo to the Federal Home Loan Bank Board. That agency began questioning Piasa about Green. As a result, Piasa cut off its loans to the developer.

Then in 1975, one of the reporters, still curious as to what had happened with that old tip they had sent the feds, gave a copy of the memo to a former head of Piasa. He thought it was interesting enough to share with James C. Green. For Green, the memo explained everything. At last he knew how and why and by whom he had been ruined. So he sued the *Alton Telegraph* for libel.

The paper argued that it had never actually printed the damaging material. The threat of libel, it said, would diminish news organizations' ability to do investigations and deter citizens from giving information to law enforcement officials.

Green's lawyer scoffed at this. Press freedom wasn't the issue, he said. Instead, the suit was about two lazy reporters who wanted the government to do their work for them and ruined an innocent man in the process. The First Amendment was no more pertinent, he said, than it would be if the newspaper's delivery truck had hit a small boy, paralyzing the child and resulting in a large judgment against it.

In July 1980, the jury returned the largest libel verdict up to then in

American history. With actual and punitive damages, it amounted to $9.2 million. At the time, the paper's net worth was $2.5 million. Unable to bear the costs of an appeal, the venerable *Telegraph* filed for bankruptcy. (It later negotiated a $1.4 million settlement.)

The nightmare of the *Alton Telegraph* is that libel suits can be filed and won for material that never appears in the paper or on the air. Simply a note, a memorandum will do. It's true that no higher court ever ruled on this case. Nonetheless, it surely has potential to be cited as precedent and that potential extends into our classroom and its Web site.

Libel laws may differ a bit here and there, but the California statute states the situation clearly: "Libel is false publication by writing, printing, picture, effigy or other fixed representation to the eye, which exposes any person to hatred, contempt, ridicule, or obloquy, or which causes him to be shunned or avoided, or which has a tendency to injury him in his occupation." For purposes of libel, publication is defined as the dissemination of the offending material to as few as three persons.

The *Telegraph* case is pertinent to you and your work. Every one of you is doing news writing for this class. You are all out there gathering news and writing it—interviewing, taking notes at meetings, reading print or electronic documents, and the rest.

Your work is "published" on our Web site and each of your stories is read by more than three people. If what you write is false and injurious or defamatory, if what you write subjects someone to hatred, contempt, or ridicule, it certainly has a wide enough audience through our Web site to qualify it as "published" and hence potentially as libelous.

Now I have checked with counsel on this. In general, you do not have much to worry about—even as other students in college classrooms do not have much to worry about when it comes to the outside world and its complaints about the work of the academy. But for that matter, professional journalists should not have much to worry about; and yet every day someone gets in trouble. If you'd like to hear about them, I'll tell you some stories of reporters who wound up on the wrong side of libel suits just by failing to pay attention to fundamentals.

There is no absolute academic or classroom privilege that protects what you write from the laws of damage and libel. If you write, falsely, that someone is a liar, an adulterer, a child molester, a dope fiend, or a mobster, and it turns out that he or she is none of the above, there may be problems.

The claim of academic freedom to protect what we do is a powerful one. So is the tradition of the classroom and its sanctity. The fact that what we do is intended for academic purposes and that we have no intention to spread or profit from the information should be a sturdy defense. But, as I said, it's not absolute—and for that I'm glad.

The constraints that apply to everyday journalists ought to be observed in our work. I think that our standards should be as high as that of any news organization. Students should enjoy no moratorium on accuracy or decency.

What does that mean for us? It means that before you write, you will have verified your information. It means you will treat your subjects and sources fairly, giving them opportunity to respond to accusations and criticism. It means that you will not knowingly present that which is not true as that which is. It means that you will acknowledge mistakes in your stories.

Most of all, it means you will understand that though journalists have vast power to do good, they also have the capacity to harm people and that you will not engage in cheap shots for the sheer thrill of it. Not now, not ever.

We are just a small journalism class, one of hundreds in the United States. But I want you to treat your work with the same care, the same concern for quality, the same respect for the abiding values and principles of our craft as if you worked for the finest paper on earth. That's what we're about, you and I. Now go out and do great things.

33

Independence from Government

To some people, it may appear that American newspapers are the servant of their government—that they report and publish stories that reflect the government's point of view. To some American journalists, it may seem as if the independence of the press is complete—that it is radically separated from any relationship to government.

Arguments can and have been made from both sides. Since the publication of *The Press and Foreign Policy*, by Bernard C. Cohen in 1963, some analysts have asserted that the press is a kind of junior partner to the official foreign policy establishment. My friends and colleagues in Hong Kong, for example, were quite critical of the way the U.S. newspapers covered the spy plane incident earlier this year. They said the papers uncritically accepted and presented Washington's point of view.

All organizations, of course, try to use the press to their best advantages. Private enterprise has its public relations experts. When industrial waste from a factory causes an environmental disaster, the PR people are on hand. This is known as damage control. On the other hand, when a company does something admirable, such as making a large donation to the local charity, the public relations apparatus tries to make sure that its client receives credit.

It is the same with government—from local to national. It wants to get certain information out and to keep other information from becoming public. They use the same tools that private industry does: press conferences, briefings, leaks, the publication of op-ed pieces, staged tours, backgrounding sessions, meetings with editorial boards, the distribution of print and video press releases and, of course, the use of spin doctors. What government cannot do, as private industry also cannot do, is order the press to present the news in a certain way. In fact, the surest way for the press to exert its independence is for government to order or try to bully the media.

But the methods I have just outlined often are quite successful enough. And often they are successful because the information is good, straight information. Not all leaks are lies. Not all press releases are fiction. Not all editorial board meetings are exercises in black information. Public affairs specialists in industry and government most often do their jobs conscientiously and I have known many that I respect greatly.

Now the success in government in being able to influence the direction of news coverage depends to a significant extent on the scarcity or availability of other sources of information. If either government or industry is the sole source of information, it stands a much better chance of having stories reported in a positive way. When other sources of information are available, the results can be quite different.

I mentioned the spy plane incident a moment ago. But let me invite your attention to the coverage—both in news stories and editorials—about the developments out of Bonn when the United States isolated itself as the only country to refuse to accept the Kyoto Accords on greenhouse emissions. Here the situation was quite different.

In this situation, journalists were well-versed on global warming and the greenhouse effect. Environmental reporters had been writing about them for years. Editorial writers had developed positions on the issues. The problem and the proposed solutions were familiar ones. Moreover, in Bonn, there was no shortage of specialists and officials from other countries and NGOs that were capable of presenting facts, putting their positions forward, and countering claims by the U.S. administration. The result was coverage that depicted the United States as standing on the sidelines while the world passed it by. The editorial commentary was largely critical. If it wasn't a public relations disaster, at least it was an event at which the administration was unable to get the press to focus on the story that it wanted.

Spy plane and the Kyoto Accords. Two important international stories with two very different emphases in the press.

The opposite view has it that the press is radically independent from government, and there certainly are important historical examples to bolster such an argument. One of these was Watergate, in which the investigations of the press, primarily the *Washington Post*, were fundamental to bringing down a president. Certainly in this case, the full power of an administration was insufficient to stop a journalistic investigation.

As his administration came under increasing fire, President Nixon and his assistants compiled a White House enemies list of some five hundred persons and organizations that had been singled out for attack. My newspaper was one of three on the list, along with the *New York Times* and the *Washington Post,* and four of my colleagues were personally identified as enemies of the president. That was a proud time for us, for it was evidence that we were pursuing our work with independence and courage.

Those who argue that the press is radically independent from government have a point. The press can be independent. It has the legal authority to be so. It has a rich tradition of dissent to draw upon. There is nothing to stop the press from being independent but the press itself. It not always is so, and on many occasions it may well appear that government and the press walk together. I want to suggest some reasons for this.

The most important of these, it seems to me, is that by and large the establishment press is a centrist one. Walter Lippmann, America's foremost philosopher of journalism, said long ago that newspapers may be a little right of center or a little left of center, but if they move too far in either direction, they are likely to lose their readers. Over the years, too, the government of the United States also is essentially a centrist one. There are Republicans to the right and Democrats to the left, but the differences between the two of them are much more likely to be measured in degrees than in magnitudes.

This is particularly so when it comes to foreign policy crises. There is an old saying in our country that politics stops at the water's edge, meaning that when great issues of national interest are involved, both parties tend to pull in the same direction. The press, being centrist in nature, reflects this. It may not continue indefinitely to reflect this. Over time, as more and better reporting is done, or when policy alternatives are clearly articulated, the press may take positions quite contrary to those of the government.

In Vietnam, at the outset, only a few papers opposed America's intervention. Mine, the *St. Louis Post-Dispatch,* was one of this small minority. In time, the press opposition to the war became much more widespread. But certainly for years, one could say that the newspapers in the United States reflected government policy.

Secondly, the press in the United States tends to reflect orthodox assumptions. There is nothing very mysterious about this. Remember when I speak of the press, I am talking about traditional or establishment newspapers—such as the *New York Times,* my own *Post-Dispatch,* the *San Jose Mercury News,* and so forth. The reporters and editors of these papers come often from middle-class backgrounds, have had traditional educations, and themselves subscribe to widely held societal beliefs.

Not many of us are radicals. Newspapers may challenge President Bush's economic or defense policies, but they do not condemn the capitalist free enterprise system or demand the dismantling of the military.

We move, in other words, within a fairly narrow spectrum, and so does the government. If it seems as if we are often moving together, it is easy to see why.

Thirdly, there is what some people call the herd mentality of the press, and which I think of as the power of the master narrative. That is, there are opinion leaders in the media—the national papers such as the *New York Times* and *Washington Post* and the big networks—and news organizations sometimes take their cues from them. By master narrative, I mean a story that gets defined in such a way and then stays that way, regardless of events.

At the time that the story of Bill Clinton and Monica Lewinsky was the leading topic in the news, you could find the press asserting that the Clinton presidency was mortally damaged and that Mr. Clinton would have to leave office. That was the master narrative. No one was reporting that very shortly, his popularity, as measured in opinion surveys, would reach historic highs. That wasn't part of the master narrative.

The relationship between newspapers and government is a crucially important—and extremely complicated—topic. The independence of the press is absolutely essential to its credibility; and without credibility we are doomed.

Nonetheless, it would be misleading to assert that the interests of journalism and government are always antagonistic, that they never coincide. But it would be equally misleading to assert that the press in my country is either the servant or the junior partner of government—or that it operates on the assumption that those who govern are always right and to be supported.

34

Serving the Public Trust

As you spoke at our first class about what you hoped from this course, the question came up: What is journalism and what is its purpose? I'll try to answer that by starting with a retired military officer named James Stockdale who ran for vice president ten years ago.

Perhaps you've heard of him, though I wouldn't be surprised if you haven't. He didn't run as a Republican or a Democrat but as the ticket mate of the independent candidate, Ross Perot, an eccentric and unpleasant Texas millionaire. I say unpleasant because I've interviewed him.

Admiral Stockdale was a war hero, an honorable man, and also a Stanford graduate (MA international relations). He spent more than seven years in a prisoner-of-war camp in Vietnam and was awarded the Congressional Medal of Honor. But as a vice presidential candidate, he was utterly forgettable. Except for one astounding moment.

In his opening statement at the vice presidential debate, Stockdale stared into the cameras for national television and blurted, "Who am I, and what am I doing here?" No candidate for president or vice president, before or since, has seemed so perplexed.

Now I'll assume you have a good idea about who you are. As to why you're here, the obvious short answer is, to study journalism or at least one form of it. But that quickly leads to the question, What is the point, or the purpose, of studying journalism—or for me to teach it?

And before any of us can answer that, we must confront the even larger question you raised: What is the purpose of journalism? So in a roundabout way, the admiral has led us back to a consideration of first principles, an excellent place to begin any inquiry. I have spent forty-five years in journalism, and I am still working out an answer. By the time this course is over, I expect to be a little further down the road, and I hope you are, too.

I've just returned from a trip to six Chinese cities and Hong Kong. Wherever I went, I talked to reporters and editors, journalism students and their teachers. In many ways, the Chinese students are like the ones I see here. They're idealistic about journalism, impatient with the status quo, and not very knowledgeable about the world.

Almost always, they would ask about the differences between journalism that is done and taught in the United States and China. There are many, and some of them are quite obvious. My answer, however, would always begin with the similarities. I would start with the purpose of journalism, for unless you have a good idea about that you can neither teach it with any depth nor practice it with any sense of direction.

The purpose of journalism, I say, is not journalism. I would ask you, as I asked them, to consider surgery. Would any of you think that the purpose of surgery was only cutting people open and sewing them back together again? Of course not. The purpose of surgery is healing.

In the same way, the purpose of journalism is not doing journalism. Knowing how to report and write are terribly important, just as developing skill with the knife is necessary for a student of surgery. Reporting and writing well are the essential skills that allow journalists to function in the service of a greater purpose.

A surgeon who talks endlessly about the value of good health but whom you would not trust to treat you for a simple cold is a worthless doctor. A journalist who knows all about theory, history, ethics, and the law of the press but who cannot go out, get the story, and write it is equally useless and ought to be in another line of work.

But for a journalist, as for a surgeon, professional skill is not an end in itself. It's a means. To what? I would say a journalism that serves the public trust. Let me explain that.

Unlike journalists who work elsewhere, those in America are blessed by the protection of the First Amendment, which as you should know says simply that Congress shall make no law abridging the freedom of the press. By a later amendment to the Constitution, the word "Congress" now means any official or governmental body, from Washington down to the smallest school board in the smallest state.

Now that protection was not written in so that a couple hundred years later press lords and transnational media corporations could enjoy annual sales measured in the billions of dollars. Nor was it written so that for the sheer hell of it, reporters could run roughshod over the rights, reputations, and sensibilities of people and later justify their vandalism as a service for the "public's right to know." Nor, finally, was it written because journalism in and of itself was an activity to be protected over farming or shopkeeping.

No, it's there because the authors of the Constitution understood that men and women to be free must be able to make their own decisions, particularly their political decisions—that you cannot have liberty unless you have access to information and that government, by its inevitable nature, strives to limit what you know. The relentless acquisition and independent presentation of that information is the public trust the press serves. The authors of the Bill of Rights considered these functions as essential bulwarks against tyranny.

You can think of this as a concept that even transcends democracy, which like journalism is only a means. Democracy is a system that is the political means to liberty, just as journalism is the professional means by which you and I can serve the public trust.

There is more to journalism, of course, than this lofty objective, and what that "more" is will be part of our conversations this year. For now, I would simply say that journalism encompasses all of life.

Ezra Pound said that the difference between literature and news was that literature was news that stayed news. By that, I think he meant more than the quality of insight or the writing. I think he meant that people have an enduring interest in the old, perpetual themes that illuminate what it means to be human. Great literature arises out of simple stories, which when examined reveal the complexities of life. In the same way, there is no subject too ordinary for journalism.

All of this relates to our subject at hand, which is public issues journalism. At the bottom of every policy, there are people. If we forget them, if we concentrate only on what "official sources say," if we go no further than the information at the backgrounder session or in the agency press release, we betray that public trust. We have not, as John Donne urged us to long ago, become involved in mankind.

We may write about the fiscal implications of tax reform, but what does that mean to men and women trying to make ends meet for their families? We may write about "the war against terrorism," but how does that affect the ways we travel, the ways we are encouraged to look at strangers, the ways in which what yesterday was private must today yield to public inspection?

As we explore the qualities of a journalism that is whole and useful, we approach a way of looking at the world and our profession that goes well beyond merely "doing journalism." We come closer to the answer to the admiral's question: What am I doing here?

That's what we'll be about this quarter—and beyond, if we are serious about this. If we are not, there are always other ways to spend a life, many of them useful and more respectable than journalism. But few of them are as satisfying and even fewer of them are as much fun.

35

To Travel Far, You Must Choose a Direction

After our first meeting, I replayed the class in my head and found that when all was said and done there were two main themes that I had emphasized. One was life, or vigor, and the other was a point of view that is based on deeply held principles.

As I thought about the first, I recalled the time I spent last summer in the Philippines, talking to groups of journalists about ethics. I had been warned that the standards there were very different from what Americans consider ethical journalism. The leading book on journalism in the Philippines at the moment was titled *News for Sale*. That seemed to say it all.

From what I could see and from the people I talked to, the title of the book was all too true. That many journalists are on the take, that they moonlight for politicians, that reporters and editors have developed elaborate systems for getting payoffs, are all acknowledged—ruefully by many of them and with indignation by the best (almost all of whom were women—don't ask me why).

The corrupt journalism has a language all its own—and everybody is fluent in it. For example, if you say "AC-DC journalism," people know you are talking about attack-collect/defend-collect. It works like this. A reporter attacks a politician and gets money from the politician's opponent. Then the reporter defends the attacked politician and gets money from that side. There is "envelopmental journalism," by which reporters get slipped an envelope of cash to make sure their stories go a certain way. There is "ATM journalism," for reporters who wish to maintain a façade of ethical behavior. They get their payoffs deposited discreetly in their ATM account.

As you might expect, the root of this evil is money. Most Filipino journalists are wretchedly paid. They may have bylines in the paper or a face on television, but they have a terrible time making ends meet. A journeyman Filipino reporter may earn 4,500 pesos a month, barely above the poverty line, which is set at 4,350 pesos for a family of six. (That's about $110 and $106 a month, respectively.) We would like to be ethical, to turn away politicians' money, they say, but we have to put food on the table.

I expected to be discouraged, perhaps even depressed, by all this, but something quite different happened. Yes, there was this awful, entrenched system, but everywhere I went I found journalists struggling for ways to regain or maintain their self-respect. I found men and women striving to do good hard reporting, which often put themselves at risk as they did it. I found them wanting to learn. I found determination to get rid of this sickness that infects the press.

Most of all, I found vitality. I found people passionate about their work. TV reporters busted themselves to beat the other station. There were a lot of daily newspapers in Manila, and the editors and reporters went after the news with gusto. Everywhere you went, you found people arguing about the news, gossiping about the latest outrage from the Presidential Palace. Newsstands were full of papers and magazines, and in a news council's office I saw racks filled with the provincial press. Journalism didn't pay much, certainly didn't pay enough, but people were finding a calling in it.

When I left, I was saddened by the plight of the journalists and the corruption that infected their profession, and I hoped what I had to say about ethics was helpful to them. But I also was moved by the energy and commitment that these reporters and editors brought to their work. They wished it could be better, cleaner, but they loved it and they threw themselves into it.

I came away energized. I concluded that I would prefer a Philippine press with venality but bursting with life to a Philippine press that was pristine but whose vital signs needed instruments to detect. With better pay, perhaps, and determination, the corruption can be cleaned up. But I do not know how you create energy and passion where people do not care deeply about what they do.

So it is with our writing. If there is energy to it, lots else can be forgiven. If it snaps and crackles and pops with vitality, people are going to read it. The trick, of course, is to bring substance and content to our writing so that it is just not all empty calories burning away. As a teacher, I can help with form, with organization, with the choice of words, with economy, with focus. But there is not much I can do to bring life to your writing. It is the commodity most lacking in editorials. That's why so many of them are so dull.

What, though, is life without a purpose, without values to guide it, without consistency? You know the answer to that, for you see it around you everywhere. You see people, some of them brighter than we, who are going nowhere. You see others whose abilities may be modest but who will travel far because they have direction. Their lives do not meander.

And so, too, it is with opinion writing. All the horsepower in the world will not rescue it if it has no place to go. You may dazzle your readers with your high-wire acts with metaphors and similes, but if there is no message there—if there is no there there, as Gertrude Stein said of Oakland—their intellect and spirits will remain untouched. You will have persuaded no one, will have started not one mind into motion. It will all have been a waste of time.

I asked you to read the *Post-Dispatch* Platform and some student platforms that previous classes adopted. The *P-D* Platform is only eighty-two words long, but for generations it gave editors direction. No one knew exactly what the founding Joseph Pulitzer had in mind when he said "never lack sympathy with the poor" or "always oppose privileged classes," but I can tell you that what the editors (myself included) did with those simple commandments was to set that paper at odds with the comfortable establishment and to maintain an arm's-length relationship with the industrial and social elite. Not many papers do that. I would not tell you that there are no alternative or contradictory public philosophies that are perfectly honorable (see the *Wall Street Journal*), but that is how we witnessed the world and it was what we tried in one way or another to articulate in what we wrote.

As a class for our editorials, as individuals for your commentaries and columns, there will need to be a point of view that is grounded in principles that matter—to us as a group, to you as individuals. Otherwise, no one will—or should—care. We will have failed as opinion writers. If we can clarify these values and bring them into sharper focus and if they can help inform your writing with conviction, we'll have done a good bit of work.

36

The Sin of Pride

There is a scene in the movie *Patton* in which George C. Scott, watching from elevated ground in North Africa, observes the German tank force moving confidently into the trap he has set. It is a moment full of tension, just before two armies in high readiness are joined in combat.

From his vantage point, Scott/Patton says, as much to himself as anyone, "God help me, I do love it so." God help me, he says, because he understands that he has yielded to the deadliest sin of all, which is pride. Though men are to die, though women and children will be left bereft, he loves it because of what he has wrought, because of how he has played the board in this terrible chess game.

I thought of Patton the evening just after our class, while I was outside grilling the peppers and eggplant and the butterflied steaks for Martha and the boys. I was walking around the garden, out by the azaleas, which she has tended so carefully. I had a gin drink, and I was thinking of our class today. (It was the philosopher Bertrand Russell, I think, who said modern man cannot survive without gin or tranquilizers. I don't do tranquilizers.)

What came into mind as I thought of our editorial board was God forgive me, but how I love it. And hardly had that come to mind but what my thoughts went to Eliot and his play, *Murder in the Cathedral*, about the murder of Thomas à Becket.

The archbishop is about to endure martyrdom, though he can yet avoid it. He wrestles with his spirit, for the temptation of martyrdom drives him to resist efforts to save himself. At last Becket says,

> The last temptation is the greatest treason:
> To do the right deed for the wrong reason . . .

Which is to say he succumbs to pride. So why do I love it so? Why did I love it above all other things I did in forty years on the job at daily newspapers? Was it the direction I could compel? Was it the control over what appeared and over what was kept off the page? Over the writers? I think all editors in the end must wrestle with this, must wrestle with pride.

I have said to some of you before that the greatest responsibility and opportunity of an editor is not what goes into the paper the next day, though that remains always a defining standard. No, I think the highest mission the editor has is the one of giving hope, of giving encouragement, of giving men and women the sense that they are about great things. I think the most profound control of all is not the control of saying this or that will happen. I think it is of setting people free to think and to express and to have done it in such a way that the product of all of this is good—in as many ways as we choose to define good journalism.

And so I thought of all of you and that tough, spunky platform that you produced and I remembered hearing you engage—on Elian, on the freedom of expression and its limits, on some thousands of truly voiceless people who are being put to the choices no civilized people ought ever to impose on mothers and fathers. It was thrilling. I mean it.

The formula is eternal. Good minds, good topics, souls that are alive and engaged—and, yes, some gentle direction. The last is where the pride enters, and there beside the azaleas I tried to fathom it, while wondering if the meat would burn, and I decided to write you about it.

Now, if you look at journalism in general—and for the moment, editorial pages in particular—you can see pride here, there, and everywhere. The Greeks hated what they called hubris, which meant wanton arrogance or insolence and which drove people to place themselves before the gods or anything else. It blinded them, and that, of course, is the tragedy of Oedipus, who would not see when he could and in the end rendered himself sightless.

In journalism, we can think of pride as the motive that produces journalism that is self-centered, that imagines that our problems and issues go to the head of the great line in which all issues and people queue up, awaiting attention or redress. That self-centeredness may be subtle, quiet rather than noisy. It may be in your face. You might have seen it this week in the *New York Times*.

Last Monday, the *Times* carried a story about a nasty piece of work by Renata Adler, the latest in the line of *New Yorker* writers to regurgitate their experiences at that magazine. Her book is called *Gone* and it's subtitled *The Last Days of the New Yorker.* People once said of Richard Nixon, accurately if not grammatically, that he hated good (and not well). Renata Adler hates good.

So in this book she trashed the late and tough federal district judge, John Sirica, who presided over the Watergate trial and more than any jurist brought the Nixon White House criminals to justice. He didn't fool around with his sentences. "Maximum John" was how he was known.

Renata Adler wrote that "Sirica was in fact a corrupt, incompetent and dishonest figure, with a close connection to Senator Joseph McCarthy and clear ties to organized crime." Now in fact, Sirica's friendship with McCarthy was well known, but no one—not Woodward and Bernstein, not any of the multitude of investigators who have ever delved deep into Watergate or its dramatis personae—has ever uncovered the slightest hint that Sirica was in with the mob. And it is not exactly as if Watergate has been unexamined. No other political scandal has received such detailed attention.

Adler offers no proof, not the slightest documentation for this apparent calumny. Sirica's family complained, but Simon and Schuster, her publisher, airily brushed it off. (The dead cannot sue for libel, so this is all about decency and ethics, not the law.) A reporter for the *Times* (Felicity Barringer, a *Stanford Daily* alum) called her on it. What was her evidence? Adler replied, "How can you be a working journalist and phrase a question as deeply silly as that?"

What about the judge's reputation? Barringer asked. "Do you worry that much about people's reputations?" Adler shot back.

Very shortly thereafter the *Times* weighed in with an editorial, which you may have read. It concluded after some meandering that only after Adler produces her evidence "will we know whether she has unearthed some remarkable evidence of historical importance or smeared a renowned jurist who is no longer able to fight back."

That is—shall we say?—measured criticism. (Our platform calls for advocacy on behalf of the voiceless, of whom surely the dead are included.) But guess what? The *Times* was unequivocal in its denunciation of Adler for her impudence toward the newspaper.

"Ms. Adler was cavalier when she dismissed as 'deeply silly' a *Times* reporter's inquiry . . . ," said the editorial, which went on to declare that "She was even more irresponsible when she asked the reporter, 'Do you worry that much about other people's reputations?' Of course we do . . . " No doubt the *Times* does, though if through some cosmic subpoena power we could call every man, woman, and child who has ever been aggrieved by the *Times'* treatment of them, we might find a witness who said the paper cared nothing for reputations.

You may drag a respected judge's reputation through the mud and get a rhetorical question from the *Times*. Talk back to it, call its reporter deeply silly, and the heavy artillery rolls out. That's pride, the placing of oneself at the head of that great queue into which all people and causes line up.

To my mind, the undocumented affront to Sirica's memory is far more egregious than a reporter being called silly. The *Times* saw it otherwise. How does the public see it? I do not know. But this I think I know; and that is every piece of arrogance on the part of journalists, which is to say all of our self-importance, comes home to roost some day.

It may come in the continued public disdain for what we do. Just as painfully, it can come when we ask ourselves, as always we must, at the end of some day, at the end of some time, whether we did our best for a cause larger than our own vanity.

The value today of our conversation was what you brought to it. Keep thinking, keep talking, keep reflecting about the principles to which we committed ourselves. Keep in mind always those readers, who are there on that great continuum from ignorance to knowledge, toward whose minds and spirits all our effort is directed. I think we can do some good journalism, if we manage to invest ourselves fully—and at the same time keep ourselves out of the way. And if you find me blindly adhering to the status quo, bring on the challenge.

37
The Limits of Free Expression

*I*n our discussion Thursday, we touched on how editors should confront columns that some readers will find hateful or offensive. The
material may be powerfully written and deal with important issues.
Are these enough to get it into the paper? If a column will hurt some
readers, should that keep it from being published, even though it will be
food for thought for others? To what extent should an editor's own tastes
control the decision?

These issues arise when editors consider columns that assert, for example, that the Holocaust is a fiction. Or that contain language objectionable to many readers. Or that mock ideals that people hold precious.
Or that disparage people for what they are rather than for what they have
done. Some of us found Mike Royko's ethnic jokes gratuitously offensive. Others thought they drove home a point worth making. How do we
decide?

Some years ago, I gave the commencement speech at the University of
Missouri at St. Louis. I remarked—only half in jest—that colleges and
universities had become the most intolerant and intellectually repressive
institutions in America. Where else, I asked, could someone be suspended for quoting a remark by a belly dancer known as Little Egypt, who
said that her art was like Jell-O on a plate? The University of New Hampshire did that to a professor (of engineering, as I recall) for using the
quote in a lecture.

Where else, I asked, could someone be threatened with the loss of em-
ployment for saying that an unintelligible take-home exam read like a
Chinese restaurant menu? That happened to a professor at the University of California at Berkeley—once the home of the Free Speech Move-
ment.

Where else but at the Fashion Institute of America, which trains its
students to perpetuate the idea that women cannot be fashionable un-

less they are anorexic, would you find a code of conduct that prohibits any message, implicit or explicit, that conveys a stereotype? That provoked some chuckles, but I quickly silenced them. At the University of Connecticut, I observed, inappropriately directed laughter can result in disciplinary action.

The real topic of the commencement speech was free expression and the official and personal limits we place on it. As journalists and editors, we are frequently faced with situations in which expression that is undoubtedly free still gives us pause whether to publish it.

Now in this speech, I referred to a book called *Tolerance,* by Hendrik Van Loon. Here parenthetically, I would note that among the roots for our word "tolerance" is the Greek word "toloneion," a toll house or custom house, which in time came to have the meaning of something that had to be endured. You can think of tolerance, then, as something that we should endure. In this sense, tolerance is necessary though not always pleasant.

Van Loon made the obvious point that there is a distinction between official tolerance (that of government or institutions) and personal or private tolerance. A good example of this comes from a famous U.S. Supreme Court decision from the Vietnam War era. A young man named Robert Cohen was arrested and convicted because he wore a shirt with the words F*** the Draft on it. The Supreme Court overturned the conviction, saying that although this message was undeniably offensive to many people, it needed to be tolerated, or endured, by society in the interests of free speech.

The Supreme Court, however, did not say whether Robert Cohen's grandparents had to endure his shirt, should he wear it to their home for Sunday dinner. The point is that what we as private people choose to tolerate is a personal decision, having nothing to do with government. Robert Cohen's grandmother would have been well within her rights to throw the mashed potatoes at him.

But what about journalists? How does tolerance fit into their professional decisions? How should an editor respond if Robert Cohen submitted a column or an op-ed piece in which he used those words to express his opposition to the Selective Service System? ("What do I think of the draft? I say . . . ") What would an editor do with Robert Cohen's vigorous and expressive opinion on an important public issue?

Actually, there is an answer to that question. When the Supreme Court decided the Cohen case, newspapers of course reported it as big news. At the same time, editors throughout the country could not bring themselves to put in their papers the word that the court said Robert Cohen was entitled to use in public (through his choice of clothing). Newspapers wrote that Cohen had worn a shirt saying "F*** the draft." Editors concluded that the language of the nation's highest court was not fit to be read by the public.

Now private people have considerable more leeway than the government in what they will or will not tolerate. That is as it should be. Official intolerance, which limits what we can do as citizens, is a greater evil than personal intolerance. Official intolerance can put you in jail, or in an earlier day get you burned at the stake.

In journalism, the question of endurance or tolerance is both a personal one and a professional one. Everyone edits with some degree of personal preference as well as with an idea of what is in the best interests of the newspaper. I say some degree of personal preference because it is important to bring just the right amount to the editorial decision.

On one hand, an editor of taste and judgment and a commitment to the great public purpose of journalism is likely over time to have developed a pretty good idea of whether something is worth printing. The editor's intuition does an effective job. On the other hand, the editor should be wary of editing too much from personal likes and dislikes. As I noted in class the other day, the demographics of this class are considerably different from the demographics of your average newspaper. My preferences and yours quite often do not coincide.

I put a lot of stuff in the *Post-Dispatch* that I disliked—that did not give me pleasure to read. I endured its publication, if you will, because I knew that if everything that went into the paper had to be liked or enjoyed by the editor, eventually the paper would find itself without readers.

But what if the editor not only dislikes something but also believes that it is untrue? It was stated on Thursday that the point of Mike Royko's column was to expose America as a nation of hypocrites. While I believe there are lots of hypocrites running around, myself among them at times, I think it's simply not true that hypocrisy is one of the defining characteristics of the American people.

So what are some tests that an editor can impose? One has to do with the author's premise. Is it plausible or is it plainly preposterous? I would have to acknowledge that Royko's premise is plausible. Does the writing meet the standards of the paper? Yes. Is the column well-organized and clear? Yes, again. Is the subject important? Surely. Does the author treat the subject responsibly? Many editors would say he did, though I would disagree.

Would the column offend and hurt some readers? I'm certain of it. Would you lose credibility by suppressing it? Probably. Someone would find out and make a point of it. It is on these matters and considerations, I would submit, that the editor makes the decision. I conclude that it's a legitimate column, though not one I'd use. (Oddly, I just learned, the *Post-Dispatch* published the column in 1999 in a set of articles on immigration. That's about twenty years after the piece was written. Those editors apparently thought it was not only good but deathless.)

A distinction needs to be drawn here between standards used for syndicated columnists and staff columnists. Most papers do not print everything the syndicates send them. That is, you subscribe to far more columnists than you can use. In the course of a week, you may receive fifty syndicated columns and have room for only fourteen—two a day. A lot of what comes in never gets published. You try to pick the best ones and, hence, it's easier to pass on marginal pieces.

With local columnists it's different. A local columnist who writes three columns a week expects to get all of them published. The readers come to expect that, too. That's where the mandate of heaven, which I mentioned the other day, comes in. In ancient China, if the emperor was overthrown, it was said that he had lost the mandate of heaven. It now belonged to the new emperor, who could rule as he wished until heaven again was displeased. In that way, dynasty led to dynasty.

So I held that columnists enjoyed such a mandate. As long as they had it, they could expect to get their columns, even marginal ones, published regardless of the topic, save under very unusual circumstances. But if over time, too many of their pieces were problem columns or if the writing simply turned bad over a prolonged period, then the editor might consider withdrawing the mandate and giving it to someone else.

Lively columns, provocative views, strongly stated opinions, perspectives that go against the grain or against conventional wisdom—all of these things can bring distinction to a paper but they provoke lots of complaints as well. And an editor braces when a columnist that works out there at the very edge of the envelope turns in his or her copy. It's a little like getting a live grenade handed to you three times a week. Sometimes the writers did this with a little apologetic smile, as if acknowledging the trouble they were about to cause you.

They needn't have—and you needn't, either, when you give your editor something that may blow up. The job of columnists is to write the best they can, with as much intelligence and style and verve as possible. Nobody ever said their job (or yours) was to make editors' lives any easier. Editors get paid to endure pieces that are worth enduring.

38
Ethical Journalism versus Journalism Ethics

*T*here was a sickening story in the papers last week about some vandals who butchered a pet hamster named Marshmallow while trashing a classroom at a middle school in Palo Alto. Reading about it, I thought of Shakespeare's line from *King Lear:* "As flies to wanton boys, are we to the gods; They kill us for their sport."

Whether the vandals were kids remains to be seen. But the wantonness of the act—its senseless and malicious cruelty—is self-evident. The power that a human being, whether child or adult, has over a tiny creature is unimaginable to the victim, and to use that power to torture and kill is a terrible thing.

Hawthorne, I believe it was, said that intentional cruelty to the human heart is the one unforgivable crime. We are talking about a hamster here, of course, not the human heart, but the point is relevant nonetheless. Deliberate cruelty, the willful infliction of pain or suffering is unforgivable. But what about pain and suffering that comes from recklessness? Are these not also the results of felonies of character? Are these ever committed by journalists?

Let me tell you about a man named Frank Prince. I should say, with some relief, that all of this took place before I had anything to do with editing the *Post-Dispatch.*

Prince was a prominent St. Louis businessman and chief stockholder in the Universal Match Company. He gave $500,000 to Washington University, back in the days when half a million meant something. The grateful university decided to name a building after him and the *Post-Dispatch* assigned a reporter to write a story about the benefactor.

The reporter found that the seventy-one-year-old Prince had served ten years in prison when he was a young man on charges of bad checks, forgery, and larceny—white-collar crimes. Very few people in the community knew that and when the story appeared, with all the awful details about a life long ago, readers were outraged. Speak about no good deed going unpunished.

Readers thought the story was a piece of vandalism—destructive, irrelevant, and certainly not newsworthy. The public did not need to know that Prince had done time to understand his generosity.

The journalistic justification for this trashing was what you might expect. The story was relevant to understanding Frank Prince and why, now many years later, he was giving back to society. Put another way, that argument declares journalists are psychologists and are qualified to assert why people act the way they do.

Another journalistic justification was the newsworthiness of the story. When somebody is in the news, as Prince was, people want to know more about them. If Prince didn't wish to have information about his life made public, he could have made an anonymous donation to the university.

You can decide for yourself which of these responses—the criticism or the justification—seems most reasonable to you. My view, as you can gather, is that the readers had it right. But regardless of where you come out on this, the fact is that journalists often have to confront the issue of newsworthiness when privacy is at stake. That's true whether the journalism is a news article or a piece of commentary, such as you are writing.

What is newsworthiness? A study not long ago by the American Society of Newspaper Editors found that there are vast differences between what the public thinks is news and what journalists consider news. The study reported a question put to journalists and readers: If the mother of a drowned child begged a paper not to publish her child's name, citing the terrible pain it would cause to read the story, should the news organization withhold it? The readers said Yes. Almost unanimously, journalists said No.

Ask a journalist what's news and you're likely to hear some version of the criteria set down by Melvin Mencher, whose book *News Reporting and Writing* is widely used in journalism schools. Mencher said that news is information about a break from the normal flow of events, an interruption in the expected. News, he says, is information people need to make sound decisions about their lives.

Decisions about newsworthiness, says Mencher, are affected by factors that include timeliness, impact, prominence, proximity, conflict, the unusual, and currency. But which of these is most important? Obviously, news decisions involve subjective judgments.

Now add to the equation the dimension of pain and suffering. Should a mother's grief over the death of her child affect our consideration of the newsworthiness of the details? Should the pain and humiliation of an elderly philanthropist be calculated into the decision about printing details of a nonviolent crime half a century ago? Here ethics enters the picture.

Students, reporters, and editors are often surprised to learn that I do not believe in "journalism ethics." That is, I do not believe there is a separate set of ethics that applies only to journalists but not other people—the baker, the butcher, the candlestick maker. I believe that there is one set of ethics for everyone, journalists included. So while I do not believe in "journalism ethics," I believe strongly in ethical journalism—a journalism that adheres to the same ethical principles by which all people should live.

This simplifies matters considerably. I've found that wherever in the world I go and whatever the audience, the relevant ethics have all been learned by the time the people were eight years old. It's not something you have to teach. People understand that you should not lie, that you should not kill or hurt people except in defense of life, that you should help those in immediate need of help, that you should respect other people, and so forth.

One important ethical precept is minimizing harm. That covers an entire spectrum of possibilities. At one end, minimizing harm means doing none at all. At the other, minimizing harm means softening the blow as much as possible when pain and suffering are inevitable. Between the two are many other possibilities.

Another ethical precept, and one that is of great importance to journalism, is telling the truth. This also is a difficult one because the entire truth at any moment is probably unknowable. What is the *truth* about welfare, for example? What is the *truth* about Iraq?

Even if journalists have done their reporting well and honestly and are lucky, all they can have are slices of the truth. Does journalism compel them to put all those slices in the story, which is another way of saying, does journalism compel journalists to write everything they know? The answer, of course, is No.

We pick and choose among the truths at our disposal to create the story. Some of the slices are left out because they are not relevant to our assignment. If you have the text of a one-hour speech by a public official, you cannot print the whole "truth" of it in a seven-hundred-word story. But relevance is not the only consideration.

Ethical decisions have to be made when competing ethical principles collide in a story. Minimizing harm is important. So is telling the truth. What if that truth is something the public should know about—the truth, say, about a drug ring operating out of the county hospital allegedly under the protection of a senior administrator? What if that truth also will result in pain and suffering, in this case to coworkers who inevitably will fall under suspicion, to family members who will suffer embarrassment or worse—ostracism, perhaps? And of course to the administrator, particularly if the reports are wrong.

How do we decide between competing ethical principles? Is it all one or all the other? I say, usually it isn't. We should craft the story in ways that both principles—minimizing harm and truth-telling—are respected, though one or the other may turn out to be more important.

The ethical journalist is always trying to navigate a way in which the important ethical principles are never neglected. The ethical journalist is always sensitive to the nuances inherent in every situation. This is hard work. It requires thinking. It requires a sturdy ethical foundation. It requires avoiding the easy, unthinking recourse to sloganeering—the people's right to know, for example. The people's right to know *what*?

But unless we journalists take on this difficult task as a condition of our work, we risk the worst outcome of all—inflicting harm, say, and at the same time failing to tell the truth that's pertinent to the story we need to tell. In such cases, people may find it hard to distinguish the journalists from Shakespeare's wanton boys who tear the wings off flies for sport. Which is how I suspect old Frank Prince felt.

39

Avoiding Stereotypes

Some of you had a lively e-mail exchange about that foolish joke told by the president of the Santa Clara County Board of Supervisors. As reported in the *San Jose Mercury News,* he likened the county spending millions of dollars on building projects to a shopping spree by the two women members of the board. They were not amused. Though he said he meant no harm, the remark reinforced the stereotype of women as people who live to shop till they drop.

The official made a similar crack about a male colleague who, he said, "likes to spend." Beyond noting this, however, the *Mercury News* reporter made nothing of it in her story. (There's always the chance that she did and an editor took it out. That's another discussion.) Perhaps it didn't seem newsworthy. Perhaps the male colleague took no offense.

My guess, however, is that the story reflected an assumption that many journalists and other people share, namely, that jokes and slurs that are directed by one member of a particular group to others in it are exempt from the same critical scrutiny that is given to such remarks when they're directed at people outside that group. A man making a joke about another man isn't a story.

Language that is scornful, even hateful, when used by outsiders is often used by members of the group itself. Frequently, journalists give it a pass. Should they? And if the answer is neither Yes nor No, unequivocally, what are the circumstances under which a journalist should respond?

Let me tell you about a couple of experiences that have taught me lessons. The first made an indelible impression on me of how deeply people can resent others using language that they casually apply to themselves.

On assignment for *Newsweek* many years ago, I covered a campaign rally for an African American congressman named Bill Clay. I'd known Clay for some time and we were (and remain) on excellent terms. On this day, the beginning of the rally was delayed and delayed. Finally, I asked the congressman when the crowd was showing up.

"Don't you worry," he said. "They'll be here. This rally's running on CPT. You know what that is?"

I said I didn't.

"Why that's Colored People's Time," he said and laughed heartily.

Later, in a different context, I used those words back to him. Perhaps I thought by saying them himself, he'd given me permission. But Bill Clay looked at me with a stare like icicles. And then very deliberately he asked, "What . . . did . . . you . . . say?" I was a young journalist then, but he didn't expect me also to be a stupid one.

The second experience was at a board meeting of the Asian American Journalists Association that I once observed in Washington. In a lull in the formal proceedings, one of the directors, a mid-level editor at a prestigious newspaper, remarked lightheartedly how much he liked to see job applications from Chinese Americans.

First, he said, he was pleased to see more Asian Americans in journalism. Second, he said that he knew the applicants would have superior academic records. But most of all, he concluded to appreciative laughter, he liked it because Chinese Americans would never cause any trouble if they were hired.

This particular hilarity either preceded or followed—I forget which— a lively and equally jocular discussion of "driving while Chinese," a phrase suggesting that Chinese Americans by nature are slower and more tentative than other drivers and thus are dangerous behind the wheel.

Now at about that very time, *Newsday* had suspended its star columnist, Jimmy Breslin, for having made racial slurs against an Asian American colleague who had criticized one of his pieces. He called her a "yellow cur" and "slant-eyed." The paper reprimanded Breslin, a Pulitzer Prize winner, but when he went on the radio and made light of it, the paper suspended him. Outraged, AAJA had asked *Newsday* to fire him.

Now there is an enormous and obvious difference between what Breslin said and the bantering that took place behind the closed doors of the AAJA board meeting. Breslin's invective was not merely insensitive, as *Newsday* chose to characterize it. He spoke in anger, meaning to hurt, using vicious, ugly words that did damage well beyond his specific target.

A racial epithet is like a shotgun blast at close quarters. Jimmy Breslin, who writes with great sensitivity and who understands the lives of people who are routinely kicked around, ought to have known it.

By contrast, the joking among the Asian American journalists was intended to harm no one. If it made fun of an ethnic group, it was their own and only their own. It was private and probably unthinking. And perhaps, in a subconscious way, it was a method of acknowledging the slights and stereotyping that these mostly young journalists have encountered in their own lives. Humor may have been the sugar-coating that made the bitter pill of prejudice easier to swallow.

And yet, I would venture that not one of them would have tolerated the same comments had they been made by colleagues who are non-Asians, any more than a black journalist will tolerate the deliberate stereotyping and making fun of African Americans around any predominately white newsroom. You can count on it that a protest would have been raised—and led, too, by AAJA—if a Caucasian journalist had regaled his colleagues with jokes about "driving while Chinese."

So what we are talking about is a commonly held double standard that goes roughly like this: It is all right to be racist if you confine your racism to your own people. In a perverse way, that is progress, for not very long ago in our history there was only one standard, and under this single standard it was acceptable for the white, male, Protestant majority to be bigoted about any other group. Such bigotry was not always risk-free, of course, and millions of decent people had no part of it and opposed this behavior; but ethnic and sexual epithets and race jokes and smutty stories were a part of the national vocabulary and discourse.

Slowly that is changing. I leave to theoreticians the question of whether we can have humor at all without whole classes of victims. The great Henry Watson Fowler notes that humor arises out of many motives, which quite often are not admirable. They are intended to hurt people or inflate the speaker's own illusions of superiority.

For example, he writes that the motive for sarcasm is to inflict pain, for invective to discredit people, for cynicism to promote self-justification, for irony to create a sense of exclusivity. By the way, read Fowler on irony and you'll never use the word again to describe any trivial oddity or coincidence.

But if we as people and as journalists wish to affect the hearts and attitudes of people for whom we write or with whom we associate, we might reflect on how we treat and use humor. If there's such a thing as the moral life of a journalist, surely one of its attributes is a desire to do what we can to help create a society in which bigotry is not a reflexive response to provocation or the motivating device for amusement. To do this, I think, it's not enough merely to protest epithets, crude jokes, and the like and to criticize or punish those who employ them.

If we wish others to stop stereotyping us, then it also behooves us not to stereotype ourselves, as the journalists at the AAJA meeting did. If we wish others to put aside racism, then we ought not to imagine that we can be racist about ourselves without demeaning consequences. People will not be valued, in other words, unless they first value themselves.

40

Narrative Journalism and Its Risks

When we discussed reported columns the other day, I mentioned that a couple years ago I gave a talk about columns and story-telling at a conference on narrative journalism. I was surprised to be invited after an article I'd written for the Nieman Reports, in which I took a skeptical view of narrative journalism. Too much of an emphasis on story-telling, I worried, may lead journalists to disregard the humbler mission of writing what happened.

But I was asked, and it was Harvard, and the more I reflected on it, the more I concluded that, handled carefully, columns could function admirably as short-form narratives. I'd like to share some of those thoughts with you in this letter, for I suspect more than a few of you have stories to tell in your columns.

I think that short-form narratives are to journalism what the short-short story is to fiction. The latter dates back to antiquity. The Old Testament is full of these little narratives. What are the accounts of the Temptation in the Garden of Eden, of Cain and Abel, of the Flood but short-short stories?

The short-short story became formalized in the nineteenth century, and it had many wonderful practitioners: O. Henry, Guy de Maupassant, Poe, Hawthorne, and Chekhov among them. Read Chekhov to understand the power of understatement.

Poe declared that these short bursts of narrative ought to aim at creating "a single effect." One also had to be able to read them quickly. The plot, character, mood, and language should be harmonious; the short-short story should reflect the unity of its elements. In time, it became understood that the short-short story (or *flash-fiction*, the awful term now used for it) should contain fewer than fifteen hundred words.

These same elements ought to be present in good columns. They should be brief. A single effect, character development, mood, language, and plot—all are important. Plot? We analyzed a column I wrote about taking a walk with my son Bennett down a Missouri creek and back. What we saw told an old, old story of nature and time. That was the plot.

What else? Dialogue has a place in short journalistic narratives as it does in short-short stories and other fiction. Point of view? Absolutely. Columns are one of the few forms of journalism in which the point of view of the author, expressed in the first person, is not a cause for raised eyebrows. A single effect? Ideas in columns are concentrated. This is not the place for discursive writing.

Action? Certainly. And here I'm not just talking about physical action—Steve Lopez's column about the wreck of a commuter train, for example—but the action that can take place within a person's mind or soul. Column writers regularly set off on expeditions into the interior, and good ones bring back treasures. But while external action can be seen or reliably described, internal action presents problems that the chaste journalist must confront. I'll return to this in a bit.

Finally, there is structure, the scaffolding or framework that gives the column its form. Like the short-short story, the short journalistic narrative ought to have a beginning, a middle, and an end that the reader easily comprehends.

You can start in the middle of the action. Where you choose to begin in the course of events you're describing doesn't matter. What matters is that wherever you start, it's the beginning of your narrative. And what comes next is the middle and then the end.

Many coaches and teachers of writing recommend a chronological form, also known as the tick-tock. They point out that it is the oldest and most familiar structure there is. *In the beginning God created the heaven and the earth.* Or, *Once upon a time. . . .*

I suspect when they figure out all that lies in our DNA, "once upon a time" will be there, deep among the other genes. The logical sequence of the clock is that of then-until-now, which is a true progression. But that is not the only logical, or true, progression. I am partial to a linear sequence, which I think of as from-here-to-there. I used it to describe that walk down Blue Springs Creek. Readers understand it as readily as the tick-tock.

There's also from-up-to-down and from-down-to-up. Jack and Jill went up the hill. You can tell a story of mountain-climbing with it. Or, metaphorically, somebody's rise and fall. There are many other such organizational sequences: from one to 10, A to Z, light to dark and, if your audience knows fine dining, soup to nuts.

People intuitively sense the logic of true progressions. The opposite, false progressions, are in every newspaper you pick up. They go like this: *The old general store had everything, from penny candy to overalls.*

False progressions can be evocative, but like euphemisms they are the enemy of clear thinking and clear writing. For what precisely lies between penny candy and overalls? What's included in that *everything*? The reader has to guess. Stay away from them.

The symmetry of true progressions can lead readers to new and distant destinations but also to familiar ones. As T. S. Eliot wrote in "Little Gidding":

> We shall not cease from exploration,
> And the end of all our exploring
> Will be to arrive where we started
> And know the place for the first time.

To help the reader know a familiar place as if for the first time is the goal of the columnist. For there are few places we can take the reader where he or she has not been before. It can be a fool's errand to try.

That goal, I would suggest, is best achieved through familiarity and simplicity, using ordinary constructions and sturdy words that have been chosen with the greatest care. We don't need the dictionary nearly so much for fancy words as we do for the ones whose meaning we take for granted, imagining that we know. In a short narrative, we have no words to waste. Every flaw—in dialogue, in plot or story, in development, in structure, in language—stands out. There is no place for the exposed writer to hide; and unlike in longer forms, there is rarely time or room in which to recover.

When I compared columns with short-short stories, I mentioned two kinds of action, external and internal. The point is important to the distinction between the literary short-short story and the journalistic short narrative.

I have quoted John Hersey's famous statement about there being "one sacred rule of journalism. The writer must not invent. The legend on the license must read: 'None of this was made up.'"

In fiction, it is made up. The fiction writer's license allows and indeed rewards the author for invention. Back in the nineteenth century, writers wanted to infuse ordinary lives with dramatic potential. In poetry, there was what Coleridge called the willing suspension of disbelief—the poetic faith that was necessary if ordinary people were to be modified by the imagination. Similarly, today editors can't get enough of what they call "real people stories."

If you agree with Hersey, none of these tools of the poet or short-short story writer to elevate the ordinary is available to you. You will have to regard invention as something as criminal as plagiarism. The latter involves theft of someone else's work. The former involves fraud—the passing off as reality something that you have made up.

Journalists can interview prodigiously and scrupulously read every document. They may imagine they know what went through their subject's mind. The subject may have told them many times what he or she thought. So may people who know the subject of your article.

And yet, journalists can never be sure. People lie under duress and for good causes. Sometimes they lie because they don't understand what really happened. And if they do not lie, they can be mistaken or forgetful. All we can truly know is what they say and what we observe. All we can know for certain is the external action.

Are we to grant columnists a dispensation because they did the due diligence before they wrote what essentially were guesses? Should we require truth in labeling, and ask that writers acknowledge what is guess and what is not? Should we simply change the name of the form—to an *interpretation* or an *impression* instead of narrative journalism? Which is to say should we let the truth alone but change the packaging?

The tools available to the short-short story writer to deepen our understanding of the human condition are many. Those available to the journalist are far fewer. To express internal action that is true is terribly hard. So be it. The last time I checked, we journalists were still supposed to be about nonfiction. The legend on the license has not expired: None of this was made up.

41

Beware the Master Narrative

Before the 2004 New Hampshire primary, the big question in the media was whether Howard Dean could resuscitate his campaign for the presidency. After Iowa, the conventional wisdom was that his candidacy was on life support, a victim of a self-inflicted wound.

Only a short time before, the media had anointed Dean as the candidate to beat, with Richard Gephardt not far behind. But Dean came in a distant third and Gephardt an even more distant fourth. The latter promptly withdrew. Dean went on television and was either (1) hysterical or (2) merely tired and hoarse, depending on whom you read.

The media quickly fastened on No. 1 and soon could talk of nothing else. Fox News pronounced him "finished." "He's done," said its correspondent, Fred Barnes.

About a week before the caucuses, the *New York Times* was reporting that "Mr. Dean and Representative Richard A. Gephardt of Missouri are locked in a tight race for first place . . . " Nobody then seriously gave the winner, John Kerry, much of a chance; and as for John Edwards, who came in second, what was he doing in Iowa at all? His endorsement by the *Des Moines Register* was regarded as quirky and quixotic.

For my part, I'm much less interested in *how* they got it backwards than I am in *why*. I have a theory and it involves what I call the master narrative.

The master narrative, as I define it, is a version of reality that is proclaimed as if in a single voice by the media. It is the instant conventional wisdom, and it often bears no relation to the reality at hand. Sometimes it is right, but often it is wrong, as it was in Iowa, and spectacularly so. It is the Emperor's New Clothes that the press whips up and peddles. It is journalism's received truth.

Here are some examples for you. When the Clinton-Lewinsky scandal broke, the master narrative decreed that the president was mortally wounded. Sam Donaldson reported that Clinton could be gone from the White House within a week. In fact, almost immediately his public support soared to record heights. Nobody in the press anticipated that. It wasn't part of the master narrative.

Here's another. On the morning after the 2000 election, America awoke to the fact that it had no elected president. Nobody knew who the winner was—and in fact, more than a month would pass before the Supreme Court handed George Bush the presidency.

Into this vacuum leaped the press, which had developed a master narrative for the occasion. The country was on the brink of a constitutional crisis. Yes!

Here was the *New York Times* somberly warning that there was a danger "that events could lurch suddenly toward political or constitutional crisis." *USA Today* concluded that the longer the recount process dragged out "the more an uneasy sense grows that a constitutional crisis looms not far ahead." From the Heartland, the *Kansas City Star* cautioned against partisanship that "could easily create a constitutional crisis that could shake this country to its foundations."

It was all nonsense, of course. A constitutional crisis was about as remote as Ralph Nader's chances had been of getting elected president. Such a crisis occurs when the machinery of the Constitution stops working. The executive branch runs wild, the legislature is dissolved, the courts are powerless, the Bill of Rights is declared null and void, and the troops leave their barracks and head toward Washington. Now that, folks, is a constitutional crisis. The Civil War was a constitutional crisis.

In the days and weeks after the election, the public kept its head. If there was a constitutional crisis in the air, nobody but the media seemed to notice it. The polls showed strong majorities—up to more than 70 percent—favoring taking the time to finish the job of the election to short-circuiting the process to get a winner by sundown. To use an old newspaper term, the public was more concerned about getting it right than getting it first. If only the editors and news directors had felt the same way.

Here's my last example. In 1997, when the British were about to hand Hong Kong back to China, my wife and I were sent by the International Center for Journalists to monitor press freedom there. When we got there, a master narrative was firmly in place. The days of a free press were over.

When the Chinese arrived, free expression would be ground under the oppressor's boot. It was ordained. Another Tiananmen Square was right around the corner. When the Chinese troops came to Hong Kong, the networks darkly intoned that the butchers of Beijing were now on the scene.

When you went to the briefings, you heard these wise ex-pat journalists and media biggies from America saying that the free press was on its deathbed. The symptoms of its demise already were visible in the form of self-censorship, which was destroying the Hong Kong press from within. Everyone agreed that journalists were afraid to do anything that might offend China.

The trouble was, as Martha and I made our way through scores of interviews and many briefings, we came upon little evidence that press freedom was flickering out. Reports of self-censorship were wildly exaggerated. Talk radio was flourishing, despite the heavily anti-China content of the shows. It ought to have been the most vulnerable media, since it could be picked up across the border in China. The main problem we found facing the Hong Kong press was not self-censorship but the savage marketplace shakeout that was killing off some news organizations and driving others to obscene lengths of sensationalism.

Now China, of course, is not exactly friendly to press freedom and the jury is still out on Hong Kong, though at the moment the media are still alive and kicking. But the point was that in the summer of 1997, the death of a free press was being reported as if it were a fact. It was the master narrative.

Now the master narrative arises from several things. A herd mentality of the press is one. The deference to the industry leaders is another. If the Big Feet are all saying one thing, the Little Feet follow along. If the reports from the *New York Times,* the *Washington Post,* the *Wall Street Journal,* and the television networks all reflect the master narrative—the assumption, for example, that Clinton was on the ropes—you can pretty much bet that this has become *the* media viewpoint.

But what allows the master narrative to take hold is a failing of independence. If we follow our Platform ("To work tirelessly and independently to present the truth . . ."), we'll be just fine.

I was telling a previous class about the master narrative, and I got a note from a student, saying, yes, she could understand the master narrative and the herd mentality that feeds it. She worried, though, that she would not have the strength to resist it. She worried about the severe pressure to conform—pressure not only from peers but also from editors who are wary of anything they aren't seeing on TV or in the big papers.

I don't have an easy answer for her question. Most of our lives are spent conforming to norms—and we would be lost or outlaws or hermits if we didn't. What makes our lives special, what can set us apart, is knowing when we need to go our own way, leaving the norm behind. It can require steely moral courage, as you readily see whenever you think about the dangerous lives of journalists in many places of the world.

So how do you resist the pressure to conform to the master narrative? I think the answer lies in what we mean when we say that someone is "centered." I think of a centered person as someone with the following qualities, which interact and reinforce each other.

A centered person has self-confidence and the courage of his or her convictions. A centered person is self-critical, possessing the intellectual humility to examine assumptions, entertain contrary ideas, and come to new conclusions. A centered person acts and is not paralyzed by arguments that cannot be resolved short of the hundredth decimal point. (Hamlet was not a centered person.) A centered person has what T. S. Eliot called a well-furnished soul and hence is comfortable within himself or herself.

If you possess these qualities you are as well equipped as anyone to escape the gravitational pull of the master narrative. If more journalists had them, the reports from Iowa leading up to the caucuses would have been a lot different.

42

Accuracy, Accuracy, Accuracy

There was a stiff little editorial in Friday's *New York Times* under the headline "On Oprah's Couch." It began by praising Oprah Winfrey's belated realization that she was wrong to defend James Frey, the author of the memoir *A Million Little Pieces,* which more aptly might be titled "A Million Little Lies." Then after a few words about the hapless author, the editorial turned its guns upon Nan Talese, Frey's editor at Doubleday.

The editorial asserted that Talese was talking "for all of publishing in the editing of nonfiction books." On one side of the gap was Talese reacting like a reader to a book and the sense of truth it conveyed. But said the *Times,* "She did not sound like an editor who was willing to stand behind the accuracy of a manuscript she had marketed as fact." In the latter respect, of course, Talese had failed—her profession, her company, her readers.

I would not argue with the *Times*'s conclusion. But it does strike me as a little fatheaded whenever I read journalists standing in Olympian judgment on lies that appear in print when journalists and readers alike have a right to expect them to be the truth—an expectation that rests to considerable degree on the reputation of the publication: Doubleday/ Frey; the *New York Times*/Jayson Blair; the *Washington Post*/Janet Cooke; the *New Republic*/Stephen Glass; the *Boston Globe*/Mike Barnacle. Ad nauseam. At one time or another, all of us have failed. If I counted up the times I was overly credulous about the accuracy of stories I was responsible for, I would be ashamed.

In our profession, and in this class, we strive for truth, knowing that it is often beyond our reach. We strive, too, for accuracy, more confident that we can get closer to it, even sometimes on top of it. Part of the problem with truth and accuracy is that for both we are often so dependent on second- or third-hand sources and even our most reliable sources—our own observations and memories—can be clouded. Nonetheless, nothing justifies our not doing our best.

In fact, the approach I urge you to take is the one asserted at the Naval Court of Inquiry after seven destroyers in 1923 ran aground in foul weather off Point Honda on the California coast. One by one, the ships followed each other to destruction. What the court declared was this: There were many reasons for the catastrophe but not one single excuse. We should think of that with the next shipwreck we find in the press or in book publishing.

The truth, as I suggested, is often, usually, beyond us, at least in its whole. Do you know that famous line from Francis Bacon, the early English essayist? *What is truth, said jesting Pilate, and would not stay for an answer.* In a way, one that is entirely untheological, that's the journalist's dilemma, but I'll get to that in a moment.

In the story that's told in the Book of John, Jesus was taken by his accusers before Pontius Pilate, the Roman procurator for Judea. Pilate asked Jesus if he were the King of the Jews, and Jesus, in effect, answered, If you say so. Whereupon, Pilate said, "What is truth?" and abruptly went outside to talk to the accusers.

We journalists often do not or cannot wait for the answer, so we must do the best we can. The answer to the truth can be large, can lie in directions we never imagine, may never be knowable. History is followed by revisionist history and more revisionist history. Each claims the truth. We journalists almost always come into the story somewhere in the middle and we leave before the end.

What is the truth of the car wreck? Where and how really did it begin? What will be its repercussions? You and I are standing along Route 10, the dead have been removed, the cars towed off the highway. We are talking to the highway patrol and later we will try to find witnesses and perhaps call the survivors. If we are accurate we may have a slice of history, which becomes our story in the paper.

All stories begin in one way or another before we are upon them. The truth may begin genetically and that particular truth may be part of an older truth that has yet to be fully realized. All truths end somewhere far in the future, if in fact they ever end. In that way truth may be like the universe. How often I wish that journalists would settle for describing their work as accurate. And yet how difficult even accuracy can be.

A few years ago the American Society of News Editors published a manual to help its members focus on "core values," which presumably were better than ordinary everyday values. In it, "accuracy" has been formally redesignated "accuracy/authenticity."

The manual said that it is as important to get the right facts as it is to get the facts right. The idea, it went on to say, is coverage that "rings true." Well, that which rings true or sounds authentic is not always what actually is true, which is one reason liars often get away with it. And besides, such coverage may well be coverage that merely reinforces conventional wisdom and stereotypes; and we can do a whole world of harm with those things.

Accuracy, accuracy, accuracy, thundered the original Joseph Pulitzer, and almost every newspaper police manual contains something similar. Accuracy is an indispensable component of truth. For while we can have accuracy without truth, we cannot even hope to approximate truth without accuracy. I started down that road the other day in class, and I hope in this letter I can take us to a conclusion.

Truth without accuracy? Some journalists assert there is something called a wider or broader truth (the new and improved truth, like these core values). To give it to your readers, you may need to make up facts or quotes or people or turn several people and their experiences into a composite.

And you've surely read about the late Senator Joseph McCarthy, whose witch-hunting against communists left for posterity the word McCarthyism—the use of sensational and unfounded inquisitorial methods. I have here on this piece of paper, he would declare, the names of ten or twenty or fifty secret members of the Communist Party who hold government office. The press would dutifully print this and it would all be accurate.

The trouble was McCarthy's statements were lies.

Truth depends on accuracy, or since truth is likely to be complex, with many accuracies. And since we journalists are more likely to be dealing in any story with a piece of the truth, or components of it, we are dealing with facts and figures and quotes and direct observations that need to be accurate.

As I said the other day, think of Vietnam and the press. Someone once wrote that it was the accumulation over time of the component accuracies about the war, in dispatches that flew in the face of the reality described by the political and military leadership, that in the end laid bare the falsity of the war, as it was being portrayed to the American people. No reporter could know the truth about Vietnam, but a reporter could be assured of the accuracy of his dispatch; and in the end those dispatches, those accumulating accuracies, brought the truth of the war to light and made it unsustainable.

Let's go to the word, and to Partridge's Short Etymological Dictionary of Modern English. "Accuracy" is a member of a large family descended from the Latin "cura"—anxiety, care, and hence the word "cure." Add the prefix "ac," and you get "accurare"—to give care to, to be careful about and hence, "accuracy" and "accurate."

If we think of accuracy or accurate as the quality of giving care to or being careful about, what do we find? We find that this is an active word, not passive. Accuracy is the result of care we have taken with something. It is not just something passive, untouched by human endeavor. It is not something that just happened.

So if we go back to its roots, we find that accuracy is associated with behavior or conduct; and if it is associated with these things, behavior and conduct, it can be evaluated using ethical principles. Evaluated not merely on the finished product—was such and such story or sentence accurate, but evaluated on the ethics of the journalistic activity that produced the finished product.

Accuracy, as you can see, can be a stretch, well beyond getting the quote right, which also is essential. As for truth, I think of it as an ideal, toward which we strive, toward which all of our work should be an important part. If we are lucky, we may even touch a piece of it.

43
Reconciling Journalism and Humanity

This will be my last letter to you for this course. We have talked a lot about journalism as it is and should be, and we have talked some about what it is to be a journalist. From everything I've said, you may understand that for me the journalist in you arises from the person you are. I hope this little story gives you a sense of how I came to feel this way.

When I visited my father's grave a few years ago in Hong Kong, one of my brothers laid a newspaper by his stone marker instead of flowers. My father was an editor, and a good one. When the book is written about journalism in China, K. T. Woo will be more than a footnote.

He was a much different editor and a much different man than I have been. My father was decisive, fast off the mark, and charismatic. He was dangerously charming and had many wives. I have brothers and sisters whom I'll never meet. At his funeral, grieving women appeared, leading their children up to the coffin to pay tearful last respects. No one knew who the women were.

But despite the different lives we lived and the different human beings we became, we were both journalists, animated by the same adrenaline rushes that come with fast-breaking news. We were both editors of large papers.

And yet, at the core we represented contrasting perspectives on journalism and life. My father saw them as quite separate, and everything in life had to yield to the imperative of the story. I see life and journalism as one, indivisible though one is subordinated to the other.

On the night I was born, half of what was then called Great Western Road in Shanghai was in flames. My father was the editor of the *China Press*. He dropped my mother off on the curb, outside the Shanghai Women's Hospital, and sped away to direct the coverage of the fire. She made her way inside alone. She, too, was a journalist but, as with many women of that time, once her child was born there was no more career.

A few years later, the war came. Shanghai was occupied by Japanese troops. Mother and I went to concentration camp, but only briefly, thank goodness. Later, the Americans bombed Shanghai and you could watch the planes high above and then see the smoke from where the bombs had hit. Then after a few more years it was over.

By then, my parents' marriage was also over, and my mother got us passage on a converted troopship—the S.S. *Marine Lynx*—back to the United States. Everyone was at the pier to see us off—grandparents, uncles and aunts, servants and friends. Everyone but my father.

When I asked where he was, someone said, at the office. He was very busy. That's the way it was in the newspaper business, they said.

For much of my life, I took pride in that. Journalism was the most important thing there was. My father's wife was giving birth, his son was going away, perhaps forever—but the newspaper business was so important that the normal responsibilities of living did not matter. I wanted to be like that, to be part of something so significant and so grand.

In time, I came to see things differently, but for a long time the question of journalism and humanity seemed not worth discussing. We followed a path that led to a Holy Grail. We worshipped at the Shrine of the Big Story. What many journalists declared as the public's right to know gave us license to take leave of all other human considerations, and if we doctored certain facts to make a better story, if people were harmed in the process, we talked of a Larger Truth.

I do not know exactly when they began to change but much of it had to do with the fact that I became a father. Late as it was, I was rejoining the human race. Those questions that had been answered on the side of journalism now stood revealed as not only monstrous but ludicrous: Cover a fire or attend the birth of your first child? Be so busy putting out the next day's paper that you cannot say goodbye to your son as he goes across the ocean?

Most of the conflicts we face as reporters and editors are not so obvious as these. The great British novelist E. M. Forster once wrote that if forced between betraying his country or betraying a friend, he hoped he would have the courage to betray England.

Rarely are we asked to choose between betraying journalism or our humanity—but if the decision ever comes I know where I would like to stand, not on the side of news but on that of humanity. But as I said, the decisions usually are not so clear. The conflict most often takes place in territory shrouded in grayness.

I should declare, however, that my bias lies with publication, with doing journalism. The arguments for shedding light, for lifting facts out of darkness and sifting them, often result in arguments on behalf of silence, of keeping the shades down, of not stirring the pot. People will argue and threaten. They will appeal to your better nature, to your sense of guilt, to anything that will keep the truth hidden.

The terribly hard part for us is to judge, to weigh, to decide. For every one hundred persons who cry wolf, predicting the direst outcome if you proceed with journalism, there is one whose plea for consideration is compelling. You need a system that both keeps you going though the deafening chorus demanding that you stop and helps you brake when that lonely, deserving voice is heard.

The hard work of reconciling journalism and humanity are too much for some reporters and editors. There are those who take refuge behind the clichés of the craft, such as asserting that the public's right to know transcends everything and to hell with the rest.

There are those journalists for whom almost any conflict is too painful—those who cannot stand the possibility of hurting anyone, regardless of ultimate benefit. Understandably, they often conclude that journalism is not for them.

The committed journalist who stays with it understands that the work is not possible without now and then giving offense, without causing pain, without provoking criticism. The journalist also knows that however carefully he or she thinks out a course of action, the approach or execution may turn out to be dead wrong. It's not surprising that so many journalists turn to strong drink and are often unfit to be around.

The conscientious journalist, in short, is not immune from the uncertainties, the conflicting values, the likelihood of error that are part of the daily possibilities of every man and woman. The reason for this is that journalism is not an end in itself but grows out of the larger life we experience as human beings. If the end of journalism were journalism, then it would be a self-contained enterprise, existing outside of society. But the end of journalism is no more doing journalism than, say, the end of surgery is only to cut people apart instead of saving lives.

The end of journalism, I believe, is to serve people in the most profound way possible. As you have heard me say, over and over, all public policy has a human effect. It will be your job to illuminate this and give your readers reliable information, arrived at by backbreaking intellectual labor and formed by judgment and guided by integrity, so that men and women can make the decisions they need to live as free human beings.

So you will need intelligence and experience to do this kind of work and also a sense of your own humanity. I simply do not believe that bad people, in the way that Socrates might have used the words, can be good journalists.

Whether you work in the news for forty years as I did or whether you do it for much shorter, the fact remains that you will be a journalist for only a part of your life. But you will be a human being as long as you live, and at the end of it all, the question of what kind of a journalist you have been pales beside that of what kind of man, what kind of woman, you were.

As I finish this evening, it is growing dark, so I think I may conclude these letters to you, with a bow to Edward R. Murrow, by saying, good night and good luck (and regards).

44
The Time Has Come

Among the columns you read this quarter were two that I wrote for the *St. Louis Post-Dispatch*. One of these was an Earth Day piece, about a walk along Blue Springs Creek that our middle boy, Bennett, and I had taken. The other was about the night my mother died. In this last letter to you, I'd like to tell you a little about how I came to write such columns and also about why I approached the form in the way I did. As you think about writing to express your own opinions, perhaps some of this will be useful to you.

On March 31, 1986, I became the editor of the *Post-Dispatch*. I was the first person to have the job who wasn't named Joseph Pulitzer and I was the first professional journalist (as opposed to a family member) to edit the paper. Naturally all of this was not only exciting but daunting as well. My experience in "managing" had been confined to the dozen or so men and women on the editorial-page staff. Now, suddenly, I was in charge of several hundred journalists and a budget measured in the millions of dollars. It was like moving from leading a chamber music quartet to directing a symphony orchestra.

Immediately, I assumed—incorrectly, as it turned out—that my most important challenge was to learn to manage. So the first thing I did was turn to my friend Dick Mahoney, who then was the chairman and CEO of Monsanto. Like a lot of business executives, Dick was frustrated in his dealings with the press. Unlike a lot of others, though, Dick was curious about journalists and wanted to know more about them. He began inviting me to lunch and we hit it off. A few weeks into the job as editor, I went to him and said, what should I do? Dick was a big-time Fortune 500 CEO, and I felt as if I were climbing the mountain to ask the guru on top for the Secret of Life.

But Dick Mahoney had nothing to say about management. In the way of gurus on top of mountains, he spoke cryptically. Always do something you love, he told me, but don't do too much of it.

What he meant was, if you love something, find a place in your life for it. If you love something, chances are you're fairly good at it, but if this thing becomes too much of your life as an editor, you will delude yourself into thinking that you are also doing the rest of your job well. In other words, love well but also wisely. (Eventually, I came to disregard his advice, which I should have followed; but that is another story.)

Immediately, then, I began to do what I loved most, which was to be a writer again. Every week, I wrote a column, and all in all, I wrote more than five hundred of them before it all came to an end, noisily, messily, and, in a way that I could not foresee then, liberatingly—all in a way that was big news in the *New York Times* and the national journalism reviews and that spilled out onto the floor of the 1996 convention of the American Society of Newspaper Editors. It was quite a ride.

What follows is the last column I wrote for the *Post- Dispatch*. In it I tried to sum up a lot of things, but mostly it was a farewell from someone who was leaving with a heart that was both heavy and light at the same time. That is a good way to leave, I think, and now if someone were to offer me that old newsroom again or a classroom with students such as you, I wouldn't hesitate for an instant. I'd spend my time with you.

Here's the column:

THE TIME HAS COME TO SAY GOODBYE
By William F. Woo
© 1996 *St. Louis Post-Dispatch*, reprinted with permission

BOURBON, MO.—From the big screened porch, where I am sitting, the ground drops sharply to the Meramec River, which at this place in Crawford County flows slow and green toward a broad sandbar below the limestone bluffs. It is a little after 6 in the morning, but already the day has heat in it. There is a slight haze, and the sun is coming over the hills beyond the river.

Yesterday, the smaller boys played in Blue Springs Creek with their pals and afterward we all kayaked, even Peter the 8-year-old, who soloed for the first time. The food, as usual, has been simple but excellent: ribs, chicken, hearty salads, melon. And just now, the music coming through my earphones is Mozart's, a little piece of choral music written when he was 15, just a few months older than our Tom.

What I am thinking is that as the world's fortunate people are measured, I am at the very top. As the world's billions of unfortunates are measured, I am not even close to being on the list. I know this, every minute of my life.

What I also am thinking about are some lines from the Book, which my mother taught me to read long ago and whose words are pertinent to everything. I am thinking of that passage about time, about how there is a season and a time for every purpose—to be born, to die, to love and to laugh and to be silent. There is, it also says, a time to cast away, which is the time to put things behind us and move on.

That time is upon me now, and I must say goodbye.

In a few days, I shall be leaving the *St. Louis Post-Dispatch,* to which I came 34 years ago. This is the last column I shall write for the newspaper.

When I talked about being among the world's most fortunate people, I had in mind not just my wife and three sons and our friends but also my work. To have had entrusted to me for 10 years the journalistic destiny of a paper edited by three Joseph Pulitzers and admired the world over has been an incomparable privilege, and for this I am grateful to the people who own the paper.

As the time came to arrange this leave-taking I had hoped to continue writing these essays. But that was a decision that in its own season and purpose went the other way, and I have no quarrel with it whatsoever. I would be lying, however, if I told you it was not a disappointment, but my disappointments in this work, all of them together, are but a bump in the road compared with the towering fulfillment that I have experienced. And this, too, I know every minute.

This has been a personal column, and from the first it was intended to be. Our newspaper had a reputation for aloofness, and I thought it would be helpful if the readers could see that in the editor there was a person not unlike themselves in many ways: Someone who knew the joys of a family and the pleasures and problems and the endless routines that come with small children; who remembered the lessons of his youth and the elders who taught them; whose mother died, as so many parents die, of a cruel disease that stole the mind before it took the body; who stumbles and takes pratfalls as he tries to walk through life. I thought it would be good if readers could come to know that whatever successes or failures the newspaper might encounter, the work in it was the effort of men and women who in their hearts and spirits were quite the same as You the people who do the millions of things that make us a country of interdependent, indispensable parts.

I wanted to look at the issues before America, but in a way that grew not out of what sources were saying or inside stuff but out of the experience of a life, which after all is the way that everyone ultimately looks at public matters. I wanted to write about journalism and the great collective purpose that lies behind everything we put in the paper. I hate the sham and pretense and hypocrisy in our business, and I wanted to expose these things so that we might concentrate on the facts and their simple presentation, without which we utterly fail in our mission of helping citizens become better informed.

I wanted to conduct explorations into the human spirit and character, to find the glories that lie everywhere therein; and in these expeditions to the interior I took along our boys: Tom, who first set out with me when he was a toddler and is now 14; and Bennett, who is 11, and the 8-year-old Peter. They have been my good companions and guides in this journey through the heart, and some of you have come to know them and have written letters about them that have meant more to me than you will ever know.

And so the boys, too, will be taking their leave. They have been good natured about letting me write about them, but perhaps it is time for them to have some privacy as they go about the work of becoming young men.

Tom is drifting away from me, as he must at this age, and I hope and wait for his aphelion, that place in a comet's orbit when it turns and begins its long return back toward the sun. Bennett's smile still summons the angels to song. I listen for their music every day. And Peter, that marvelous work in progress, is unfolding his mysteries in ways that fill us with laughter and wonder.

The other day, he observed that our names actually determine who we are. "I'm really a Peter," he told his mother, "and Bennett is really a Bennett, and Tom is really a Tom." And then he paused and said, "If you and Dad had only named me Elvis, I'd be really cool."

Boys, boys . . . hurry. Take my hand. There's a street to cross and a world beyond it. No more dawdling for us here.

Below me, the Meramec flows old and slow and green, coming from somewhere else, now approaching a bend under high limestone and then going on its way, toward another place that cannot be seen from here. It is a still, peaceful morning, and this is the time. I wish you all the best there is.

And to you, my good students, I also wish you all the best there is.
Regards, Bill Woo

Index

About the Author

William F. Woo
(1936–2006) was
the Lorry I. Lokey
Professor of
Journalism at
Stanford University.

About the Editor

Philip Meyer is Knight Chair and Professor of Journalism at the University of North Carolina at Chapel Hill. He is the author or coeditor of a number of books, including *The Vanishing Newspaper: Saving Journalism in the Information Age* and *Assessing Public Journalism*, both available from the University of Missouri Press.